ESPN: One Giant Leap For Fankind

A Walk Through Sports History With the Man Who Changed It

Bill Rasmussen
Founder of ESPN

with
Donald T. Phillips

Headline Books
Terra Alta, WV

ESPN: One Giant Leap For Fankind
A Walk Through Sports History With the Man Who Changed It

by Bill Rasmussen
with Donald T. Phillips

To order additional copies of this book or for book publishing information, or to contact the author:

Headline Books
P.O. Box 52
Terra Alta, WV 26764
www.HeadlineBooks.com
mybook@headlinebooks.com

Book cover design and copy by ESPN Creative Studio

ISBN 13: 9781958914069

Library of Congress Control Number: 2022946687

PRINTED IN THE UNITED STATES OF AMERICA

It's never been a habit for ESPN to look back on our achievements – we're about what's next. There's much left to be done for us to serve sports fans every minute of every day - anytime, anywhere and on any platform. That ferocious dedication to bettering ourselves is just one of the things that makes us special.

The opportunity to share this wonderful book from our founder, Bill Rasmussen, with the entire ESPN team allows me to reaffirm our collective appreciation for everything Bill means to us. What he and his son Scott concocted in a 1976 Mazda GLC on a Connecticut highway in 1978, and boldly launched in 1979, remains one of the all-time success stories. Their dream is the reality we collectively share in protecting and growing.

Bill and the pioneers who joined him in starting ESPN were most certainly sports fans. It was their sports mentality that infused what remains in our DNA today - hard work, collaboration, innovative thinking and boundless creativity.

Two things struck me when reading this book. First, Bill did a remarkable job of describing the media and sports landscape from his Chicago childhood through today, and he intertwined ESPN's indelible place in that history.

Second, I was struck by just how much Bill valued each one of his teammates. He never took for granted the consistency with which he encountered – and hired! – driven risk-takers who were never complacent. They reached beyond the possible every day, much like we continue to do in a rapidly evolving world with plenty of uncertainty and challenges of its own. Obstacles never limited us before and won't now. And for that, we have Bill Rasmussen to thank.

Bill, without you, ESPN obviously wouldn't be here today. I speak for all our employees when I say we are grateful for all that you have done and continue to do – we will always do everything we can to honor your legacy and your impact.

Jimmy Pitaro

Dedicated to sports fans everywhere.
You made my dreams come true.
Thank you!

Acknowledgment

I deeply appreciate the countless hours Lynn Daniels devoted to bring this book to completion. Her comments and suggestions, editing and visualization skills, patience and, yes, tolerance for my many quirks, made it all possible.

Cover Design

In 1844, Samuel Morse transmitted a message from Washington, DC to Baltimore via telegraph. That was the beginning!

By the time I was born in 1932, we had the radio (Marconi), the telephone (Bell), Edison invented the light bulb, Duryea the automobile and the Wright Brothers began to fly. RCA began developing television in 1929.

On a parallel path, America's passion for sports grew: Baseball began in 1846 and the first World Series was played in 1903. The first college football game between Rutgers and Princeton was in 1867, the Rose Bowl in 1902, and the National Football League was formed in 1930. Basketball was invented by James Naismith in 1895.

Our country had a Civil War (1865-1869), a World War (1917-1918), the stock market crashed in 1929, and we lived through the Great Depression from 1929 to 1936.

During my early years, the collegiate and professional sports teams rejected both radio and television. Most of the teams thought their fans would stay away from stadiums if they could listen to the radio/TV for free.

From the late 40s through the late 70s, life changed dramatically. Cable TV was introduced, color TV was new, and Neil Armstrong walked on the moon. In 1975 RCA Americom launched Satcom I and ESPN launched around the clock coverage of nothing but sports in 1979.

The cover, designed by ESPN Creative Studio, gives the reader a glimpse at the roadmap through history from the telegraph to today's massive worldwide coverage of sports.

Description of cover art:

- **Front cover** shows 3 lines that are weaved throughout the book. The **first** is Bill Rasmussen's life story, memories, hopes and dreams that span 10 decades from the year he was born to today. The **second** is the changes in sports and the **third** shows the changes in technology.
- From 1844 to 1932, **technology** was developed that laid the groundwork that made ESPN possible. That short stretch on the timeline reached its pivot point, made an abrupt turn and exploded: first with technology, much of it developed along with the Space program, followed by **sports**.
- **Morse code** begins the timeline 88 years before Bill is born. The timeline extends another 88 years to today.
- **The turning point** has circular **radio waves** as the grey timeline comes to Bill's year of birth in 1932. Here, the timeline takes a quick turn upwards, representing the acceleration of new technologies like the black and white television.
- The grey timeline changes to **colors** that match the red, green, blue (RGB) used in the original color TV sets.
- **Space walker** is the ultimate sports fan wearing 79 on the space suit for the year ESPN went on the air, carrying the ESPN flag, floating between the **moon** and the **satellite**.
- The book Title and Dedication reflect how much Bill appreciates the fans.
- **Back cover** shows a **silhouette** of the one man who made it all happen: Bill Rasmussen.
- **Spine includes a fan favorite #1 foam finger.**

Book cover design and copy by ESPN Creative Studio

Table of Contents

Walk with me into the future with
Intentional Optimism

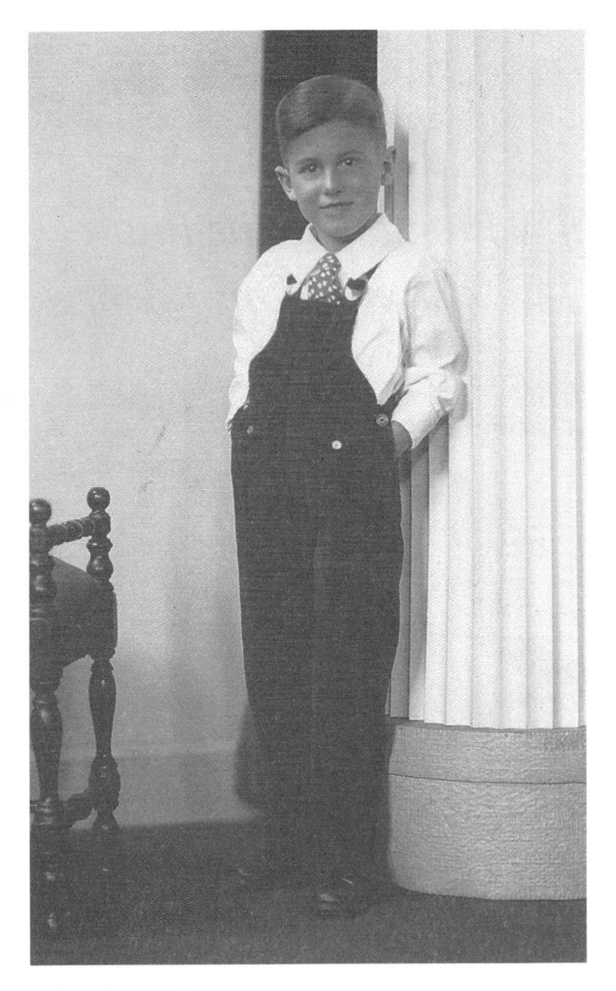

Bill in first grade

Introduction

When I was five years old, my grandfather started talking to me about baseball. His name was Frank O'Connor. He was an Irishman, he was my mom's father, and he was a White Sox fan – probably in that order. As a young man he worked for the Post Office in Chicago. I remember him telling me that he ditched work so he could go to the 1906 World Series between the Cubs (North Side) and the White Sox (South Side). It was, and still is, the only time the two Chicago teams played each other in the World Series. That year, they alternated fields – game one at the West Side Grounds (Cubs), game two at South Side Park (White Sox), and so on. [This was before Comiskey Park (1910) and Wrigley Field (1914) were built.] The visiting team won every game except the last one. My grandfather saw every pitch. And he told me all about it.

Grandfather Frank O'Connor (L) and Bill Rasmussen at age six (R)

The mighty Chicago Cubs had won 116 games in the National League that year, had the best pitching staff in baseball, and were heavily favored. The Chicago White Sox were called the "Hitless Wonders" because they had the worst team batting average in the American League. But they had gone on a late-season 19-game winning streak to win the pennant. There were colorful players, such as pitcher Mordecai "Three Finger" Brown and the trio of Joe Tinker (shortstop), Johnny Evers (second base), and Frank Chance (first base) who were the best double-play combination in baseball (known as the great Tinker-to-Evers-to-Chance.)

But in one of the biggest upsets in sports history, the White Sox beat the Cubs in six games. The score of the final game was 8-3, it was played on the White Sox home field, and my grandfather was in baseball heaven. Thirty-one years later, his enthusiasm in describing that World Series to me made it seem like he was actually back in time watching the games again.

And that's where my love of sports began.

Bill Rasmussen

Prologue

Can you imagine any possible connection between the World Series of 1906 and the launch of ESPN in 1979? Well, there is. It went from my grandfather to me to the average sports fan – kind of like Tinker-to-Evers-to-Chance. My grandfather's stories of that World Series sparked in me a love of sports that has lasted a lifetime. And without that, there would have been no ESPN.

In 1906, there was no radio or television or anything else, for that matter. You either had to go to the game or read about it in the newspaper. The fastest communication technology of the day was the telegraph. In 1844, when Samuel Morse sent his first message from Washington, D.C. to Baltimore, he revolutionized long-distance communication. During the Civil War, Abraham Lincoln used it to communicate with his generals in the field (rather than sending couriers). Lincoln also initiated plans to lay a telegraph cable across the Atlantic Ocean from the United States to Europe, which was completed in 1866.

It took another half-century for Guglielmo Marconi to file his patent for the radio (1897). Nine years later, on Christmas Eve 1906 (a few months after the World Series), inventor Reginald Fessenden made history by broadcasting music and speech via radio waves from Massachusetts. This new technology was originally called "wireless telegraphy." In short order, the U.S. Navy built the first major radio facility near Washington, D.C. and began broadcasting daily time signals and weather reports – in Morse Code. And when World War I rolled around, radio was being used by the military, largely to communicate with airplanes.

The "War to End All Wars" ended at the 11th hour of the 11th day of the 11th month in 1919. But instant mass communication was just getting started.

History shows us that new developments in communications technology were first utilized during wars and in sports. And every time, the old technology was employed to transition to the new. For example, the first live broadcast of a baseball game over the radio took place on August 5, 1921, when the Philadelphia Athletics visited the Pittsburgh Pirates. [The Pirates won 8-5.] While the players were there, the announcers weren't anywhere near the ballpark. They were sitting in the radio station's studio receiving play-by-play accounts over a telegraph wire. Then they would spice up the calling of the game using their imagination and enthusiasm. There were also baseball "viewing parties" held in bars and theaters where a large board with mechanical players had to be moved physically with each play. The board also had a light-up section that kept track of balls, strikes, and outs. Updates for these games were made by using, you guessed it, the telegraph. Large corporations didn't get involved in the radio business until the 1920s. And live radio sports broadcasting really took off after World War II.

The Greatest Generation won the second world war for us. I'm a member of what is called The Silent Generation (born between 1925-1945). [After the war, of course, came the Baby Boomers.] I've been fortunate enough to live through an amazing evolution of technology, which has been unprecedented in human history. Just think about it. The time span from the invention of the telegraph in 1844 to 1932 (the year I was born) was 88 years. During that time, mass communication advanced from the telegraph to the AM radio – and that's it. On October 15, 2020, I turned 88. During my lifetime, mass communication technology has gone from AM radio to the transistor radio to broadcast television to cable television to satellite communications to the iPhone to live streaming via the Internet. Sports have changed and grown with each of those new inventions. And I have witnessed it all and participated in some of it.

So walk with me now through those 88 years. Along the way, I've related part of my own personal journey, noted some major events in American and sports history, and made a few personal observations. Each chapter in this book covers a decade with a scorecard and a list of champions at the end. See what was happening when you were born and when you were a kid growing up. Check out some history involving your favorite teams. Watch the technology stair-step up to where it is today. And read how the growth of technology took sports – the games we watch and play – to new and unimaginable heights.

One of the things I've seen over these many years is that sports just keeps on going and growing. Year in and year out, month in and month out, there are heroes and goats, tough losses, and big wins. We *love* sports. We *need* sports. Even a pandemic can't stop sports for long. *Sports* are part of the American psyche. And I'm proud to have played a small part in advancing the games.

Babe Ruth

The 1930s

If you had to sum up the decade of the 1930s in one word, it would be (as Yogi Berra might say) "The Great Depression." On October 24, 1929, in what was called Black Thursday, the stock market crashed. The slide continued three days later on Black Monday (October 28, 1929). By 1932 the market had dropped to its lowest point of the 20th century – a full 89.2 percent loss in three years. That was the year I was born.

The Depression was as much mental as it was financial. People were not feeling good about themselves. When Franklin D. Roosevelt assumed the presidency in 1933, he took control. Over the next six years, he implemented the New Deal to get everybody out of the doldrums, put them back to work, provide financial support, and enact new laws for future protection (including Social Security in 1935). At its worst, the unemployment rate soared to 24.9 percent, which translated into 15 million people being out of work. My father was one of them.

Dad was born in 1908 and had broken into the banking business as a runner in Chicago's downtown financial district. Back then, of course, there was no electronic way to transfer checks, so it had to be done physically. Three or four times a day, he would take all the checks that had been written in one bank and get them to the bank on which the check was to be drawn. He had worked his way up to assistant bank teller when, in 1932, he was laid off. Soon after I was born, my parents moved in with my grandmother. After a short while, we moved into an apartment for a year. And then my father and uncle built the small house I grew up in. My mother was a stay-at-home mom. I had two brothers born in the '30s and a sister in 1940. To make ends meet for his growing family, Dad delivered glass bottles of milk at 4 o'clock in the morning, and became a streetcar conductor for the Chicago Transit Authority. I remember one hard and fast rule he had. "We'll figure out how to feed everybody. But I don't ever want to see a scrap of food left on your plate. Take what you want. Make sure you get as much to eat as you need. But don't ever leave anything on your plate." It was almost a threat.

Today, we think of Chicago as a massive metropolis. But in those days we lived on the southwestern outskirts where the city had been expanding. A couple of blocks south of our house was a large swamp that would freeze over in the winter. That's where my dad taught me to ice skate. To me, it was the largest skating pond in the world. You could literally skate for miles. We lived on 96th Street, near a larger two lane road that is now a major interstate. When I started first grade in 1938, my mother could stand on the front porch and watch me walk the entire half-mile to school. Our building was made of concrete and brick and it had four rooms. Grades one through eight were taught there. The big kids were taught in the two rooms upstairs and the little kids had the two rooms downstairs.

I was a baseball player from day one and this little school was where I got started. Kids baseball was organized by grade school or high school. And we played each other in the Chicago area. All the schools were small. In fact, we only had 150 kids in ours. But we had a lot of fun as teachers and parents were usually very involved. Formal Little League began at the end of the decade (in 1939).

Back then, baseball was America's pastime. It was the one sport everybody seemed to talk about and many people kept track of their favorite team and all the players on it. In Chicago, everybody loved either the Cubs or the White Sox. In the '30s, the White Sox had future hall-of-famers Luke Appling, Ray Schalk, Al Simmons, and Ted Lyons. At Wrigley Field, the Cubs had the likes of Rogers Hornsby, Hack Wilson, Gabby Hartnett, and even Dizzy Dean (for a few years). One of the biggest things that happened during the '30s was Babe Ruth's called shot during the 1932 World Series (in Chicago). But most sports fans also followed what was going on around the country, as well. We all knew the Babe played one of his last games in Pittsburgh in 1935 during which he hit three homes runs and went four-for-four with six RBIs. The Babe's last home run (#714) literally was hit out of the park – the first time that had ever happened at Forbes Field. As Ruth was bowing out, Joe DiMaggio (1936) and Ted Williams (1939) were making their debuts. And every sports fan knew that Johnny Vander Meer had pitched back-to-back no-hitters for the Cincinnati Reds in 1938.

The truth is that, in the decade of the 1930s, sports exploded onto the American scene. While FDR's New Deal programs were trying to pick up everybody's spirits, sports started expanding for exactly the same reason. It was entertainment – and much-needed relief from all the pain, anguish, and suffering of the Great Depression. In Chicago, Arch Ward (sports editor for the Chicago Tribune) came up with the idea for a Major League All-Star game as part of the 1933 Chicago World's Fair. It was billed as the "Game of the Century" and the next year was called "The Midsummer Classic." The American League won that first game 4-2 at Comiskey Park with Babe Ruth hitting a two-run homer in the bottom of the third inning. Of the thirty-six players who played in that first All-Star game, twenty were elected to the Hall of Fame.

Arch Ward also came up with the idea to play the first College All-Star Football Classic, which pitted the National Football League champs against a team of star college players. That first game was played in 1934 at Soldier Field in Chicago and continued as a preseason tradition right up until 1976. College football, in general, also expanded greatly. Prior to the 1930s, the Rose Bowl was the only post-season extravaganza. Four more New Year's Day games also were born in that decade: The Orange Bowl, the Sugar Bowl, and the Sun Bowl (all in 1935), and the Cotton Bowl (in 1937). Also, in 1935, the first Heisman Trophy was awarded by the New York

Heisman Trophy

Downtown Athletic Club. The first winner was University of Chicago halfback Jay Berwanger.

There were two forms of mass communication at the beginning of the decade: 1) Newspapers, which were delivered to everybody's front doorstep and 2) Radio. In the 1920s, AT&T had signed a deal with RCA to use its wire infrastructure for radio. RCA then formed the NBC radio network. CBS was formed shortly thereafter and local radio station affiliates began springing up around the country. At the beginning of the decade, 12 million households owned a radio. By 1939, it was 28 million. In 1934, a group of independent stations joined together to form the Mutual Broadcasting System and broadcast syndicated radio entertainment programs, such as *The Lone Ranger*. Historically, the decade of the 1930s was known as the Golden Age of Radio.

Radio broadcasting in sports lagged behind the general national trend in the '30s largely due to the fact that baseball team owners resisted attempts to broadcast their games fearing that if the fans could listen to a game on the radio, they would not go to the ballparks, which would then result in a loss of revenue. Essentially, the teams instituted radio bans, especially for home games. However, in 1935, Major League Baseball signed a deal that allowed the World Series to be broadcast on all major networks. And by 1939, all major league teams were broadcasting on the radio, with certain limitations.

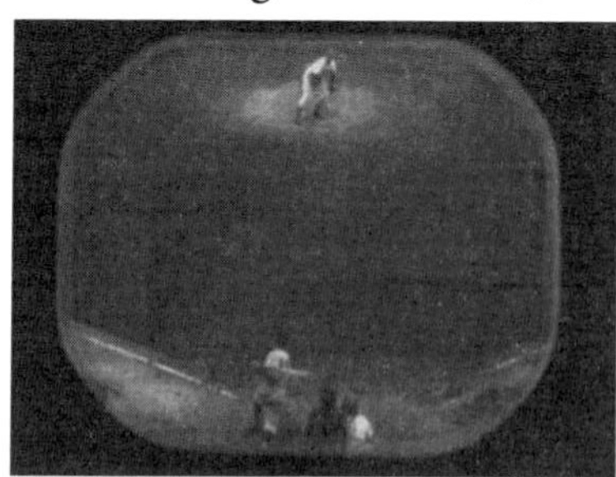

First professional televised baseball game between the Reds and the Dodgers

The first televised baseball game took place on August 26, 1939, as part of the New York Worlds Fair. Television was one of the fair's prize exhibits and it was broadcast by Station W2XBS (later to become WNBC) in New York City. The game was between the Cincinnati Reds and Brooklyn Dodgers at Ebbets Field in Brooklyn. Red Barber called the game as the Dodgers defeated the Reds 6-1. At the time, there were only a couple of hundred television sets in New York. However, the World's Fair provided a catalyst for developing television technology. The upside potential for revenue generation by selling advertising and broadcast rights became obvious to those in the sports world.

As we were moving toward the turn of a new decade, Japan was at war with China. And on September 1, 1939, the Germans invaded Poland.

Scorecard: 1930s

U.S. Population	123 million
President	Herbert Hoover Franklin D. Roosevelt
Major Events	The Great Depression (1929-1939) Gandhi's Salt March in India (1930) Roosevelt's New Deal (1933) Prohibition Repealed (1933) Adolph Hitler becomes Chancellor of Germany (1933) Social Security (1935) Hindenburg Disaster (1937) Amelia Earhart Disappearance (1937) World War II Begins (1939)
Most Popular Sport	Baseball
Sports Events	Babe Ruth's Called Shot in the World Series (1932) 1st Night Baseball Game, Cincinnati (1935) Jesse Owens Wins Four Gold Medals in Olympics (1936) Joe Louis wins Heavyweight Boxing Title (1937) 1st NCAA Basketball Tournament (1937) 1st Baseball Game Broadcast on Television (1939) Lou Gehrig's Farewell Speech (1939)
Sports Additions	1st Playing of National Anthem at Olympics (1932) Baseball All-Star Game (1933)

	College All-Star Football Classic (1934) 1st Heisman Trophy (1935) 1st Olympic Torch Relay (1936) Orange, Sugar, and Sun Bowls (1935) Cotton Bowl (1937) Little League Baseball Founded (1939) Baseball Hall of Fame (1939)
New Technology	[RCA Begins TV Development (1929)] 1st Radio broadcast of Olympics (1936) CBS Begins TV Network (1937) 1st Televised Major League Baseball Game (1939)
Communications	Newspapers Radio
Average Baseball Ticket Price	$ 1.00

The Champions

MLB World Series

Year	Champion	Result	Opponent
1930	Philadelphia Athletics	(4-2)	v. St. Louis Cardinals
1931	St. Louis Cardinals	(4-3)	v. Philadelphia Athletics
1932	New York Yankees	(4-0)	v. Chicago Cubs
1933	New York Giants	(4-1)	v. Washington Senators
1934	St. Louis Cardinals	(4-3)	v. Detroit Tigers
1935	Detroit Tigers	(4-2)	v. Chicago Cubs
1936	New York Yankees	(4-2)	v. New York Giants
1937	New York Yankees	(4-1)	v. New York Giants
1938	New York Yankees	(4-0)	v. Chicago Cubs
1939	New York Yankees	(4-0)	v. Cincinnati Reds

NFL Championship

Year	Champion	Result	Opponent
1930	Green Bay Packers	*	v. New York Giants
1931	Green Bay Packers	*	v. Portsmouth Spartans
1932	Chicago Bears	*	v. Green Bay Packers
1933	Chicago Bears	(23-21)	v. New York Giants
1934	New York Giants	(30-13)	v. Chicago Bears
1935	Detroit Lions	(26-7)	v. New York Giants
1936	Green Bay Packers	(21-6)	v. Boston Redskins
1937	Washington Redskins	(28-21)	v. Chicago Bears
1938	New York Giants	(23-17)	v. Green Bay Packers
1939	Green Bay Packers	(27-0)	v. New York Giants

**NFL 1930-32 scores disputed*

NHL Stanley Cup *

Year	Champion	Result	Opponent
1930	Montreal Canadiens	(2-0)	v. Boston Bruins
1931	Montreal Canadiens	(3-2)	v. Chicago Blackhawks
1932	Toronto Maple Leafs	(3-0)	v. New York Rangers
1933	New York Rangers	(3-1)	v. Toronto Maple Leafs
1934	Chicago Blackhawks	(3-1)	v. Detroit Red Wings
1935	Montreal Maroons	(3-0)	v. Toronto Maple Leafs
1936	Detroit Red Wings	(3-1)	v. Toronto Maple Leafs
1937	Detroit Red Wings	(3-2)	v. New York Rangers
1938	Chicago Blackhawks	(3-1)	v. Toronto Maple Leafs
1939	Boston Bruins	(4-1)	v. Toronto Maple Leafs

**NHL 1930 best of three 1931 - 1938 best of five 1939 - present best of seven*

The Champions

NCAA College Football

1930	Alabama / Notre Dame
1931	USC
1932	USC
1933	Michigan
1934	Minnesota
1935	Minnesota
1936	Minnesota
1937	Pittsburgh
1938	TCU
1939	Texas A&M

Heisman Trophy

1930			
1931			
1932			
1933			
1934			
1935	Jay Berwanger	RB	Chicago
1936	Larry Kelley	End	Yale
1937	Clint Frank	HB	Yale
1938	Davey O'Brien	QB	TCU
1939	Nile Kinnick	HB/QB	Iowa

NCAA College Basketball

1930		
1931		
1932		
1933		
1934		
1935		
1936		
1937		
1938		
1939	Oregon	(29-5)

Ted Williams

The 1940s

Just as the 1930s were defined by the Great Depression, the 1940s were marked by the beginning and end of World War II. I was nine years old and in the fourth grade when the Japanese bombed Pearl Harbor. The next day, my father sat us all down in front of the radio to hear FDR's speech to the nation. "You have to listen to this," he said. "It is really, really important." I can still hear as clear as a bell the President's first sentence: "Yesterday, December 7, 1941 – a date which will live in infamy – the United States of America was suddenly and deliberately attacked by naval and air forces of the Empire of Japan." And I'll never forget his closing, "We will gain the inevitable triumph, so help us God." My mother got up and went into the hallway so the children would not see her crying.

We didn't have much of an army then, and everyone expected the Japanese to start bombing the west coast. A few days later, when Germany declared war on us, there was a very real concern that they were going to attack the east coast. The nation saw an incredible burst of patriotism as hundreds of thousands of Americans enlisted in the armed forces. My father went down to the draft board and registered. But because he was born in 1908 and had four children, they told him to go home and take care of his family. The war very quickly ended the Depression as production for the war effort ramped up and jobs became plentiful. In Lake Forest, Illinois, we were making torpedoes. In Manitowoc, Wisconsin, we were producing submarines and launching them in Lake Michigan, where they were towed down through the Chicago River, out to the Mississippi, and down to the Gulf of Mexico. Also, in the Midwest, we built planes, ships, guns, tanks, and aircraft engines. My father got a job at the Dodge Chicago procurement office where we were making aircraft engines for B29s. The campus where he worked took up thirty city blocks on the South side.

Nearly everybody who wanted a job was able to find one. Hundreds of thousands of women joined the workforce and, after some negotiating, received the same wages as men. Almost forgotten today is the fact that there were thousands of labor union strikes during the war (3,742 in 1943 alone). All the strikes were viewed as very unpatriotic, especially by our servicemen overseas, one of whom said: "We're getting sick and tired of reading about strikes at rubber plants and coal mines back home. They make in a week what we are paid in a month." FDR pretty much ordered the companies to settle with the workers to get them back to work. If they needed more money, the federal government gave it to them.

At home, both gas and food were rationed, and my mother, especially, was very concerned about food availability and being able to feed her four kids. So, in our back yard, we put in one of America's 20 million "Victory Gardens," which produced an estimated 40 percent of food during the war. We grew corn, beets, carrots, tomatoes, and lettuce.

Also, as part of the war effort in Chicago, we all had to put up blackout curtains. There were air raid wardens, air raid sirens, and drills. Small Piper Cub planes would fly over neighborhoods to see if people were appropriately blacking out.

It was in the early 1940s when I really became interested in history. There was no television back then, and radio really ramped up news coverage. We read major headlines in the newspapers whenever a big event occurred. I remember the Chicago Tribune printing progress maps of American movements in Europe and the Pacific. And on Saturday afternoon at the movies, they showed a War Department 15-minute summary of what had happened in previous weeks. Early in the war, much of the news was censored by the government, largely because it was not good. But that quickly turned around. On April 18, 1942, for instance, Jimmy Doolittle and his Tokyo Raiders managed to get their large B-25 bombers to take off from the aircraft carrier USS

Hornet and successfully bomb the Japanese mainland. Then, almost exactly six months after Pearl Harbor (June 4-7, 1942), the four Japanese aircraft carriers that launched the December 7 attack were sunk at the Battle of Midway. And exactly one year after the Doolittle Raid (on April 18, 1943), Japanese Admiral Yamamoto, who had planned the attack on Pearl Harbor, was killed when his plane was shot down over the Solomon Islands.

Sports, for the most part, carried on as usual. In the summer of 1942, my grandfather first started taking me to baseball games at Comiskey Park. So, of course, I became a diehard White Sox fan. Eventually, I boarded the streetcar by myself and traveled a few blocks to the ballpark – usually being one of the first people they let into the park. Almost right away, many pros started going off to war. Bob Feller joined the Navy, Joe DiMaggio and Hank Greenberg, the Army, and Ted Williams became a Marine/Navy pilot (to name just a few). When the Commissioner of Major League Baseball asked FDR if the season should be suspended for the duration of the war, the President, with his famous Green Light Letter, basically said "Play Ball" and even asked for more night games so day shift workers could attend.

Bob Feller

I remember when President Roosevelt died on April 12, 1945. People were terribly shocked and saddened. And while the country mourned, everybody was worried about Harry Truman's ability to lead. History shows they needn't have been. Within five months of Truman taking office, both Germany and Japan had surrendered – the final daggers, of course, being his order to drop nuclear bombs on Hiroshima and Nagasaki. Our family was in Lake Ripley, Wisconsin, that summer and we started hearing car horns blowing and people yelling when the Emperor of Japan announced his country's surrender.

After the end of the war in Europe, General Patton realized that there were a lot of baseball players in the service, so he staged the Armed Forces World Series in 1945. Several of the games were played at the Hitler Youth Stadium in Nuremberg, Germany. As the ballplayers came back from the war, they were treated as returning heroes, and rightly so. The cheering at Comiskey Park was deafening each time one of our veterans came to bat. Williams, DiMaggio, Feller, Hank Greenberg, and many more – we saw them all play.

Bill (R) as a cadet commander in Armed Forces Day Parade

I started high school in 1946 and, by 1948, I was the cadet commander in the Army ROTC. To honor our veterans, our corps participated in Armed Forces Day parades along Michigan Avenue in downtown Chicago. There were bands playing, flags waving, and thousands of people cheering along the way. And back then, many of us carried M1 rifles as we marched.

In 1948, the Chicago Sun Times ran an essay contest for high schoolers, which I entered and became one of the winners. The prize was a trip to Washington D.C. to attend the inauguration of Harry Truman who had upset Thomas Dewey in the presidential election. (I still vividly remember Truman holding up the front page of the Chicago Tribune with the headline "Dewey Defeats Truman.") Six kids from Chicago sat in the grandstand as the guests of Illinois Senator Paul Douglas. We stayed at the Shoreham Hotel and were invited to the inauguration ball there. General Omar Bradley came up to me, introduced himself, and said, "Having a good time, young man?" All I could manage to get out was, "Yes, sir."

I played baseball all through high school. The 36 high schools in the Chicago area were divided into four divisions – North, South, East, and West. In our division, there were four all-white schools, four all-black schools, and one mixed school. It was a pretty simple time back then. We played each other at home and away. For away games, the players were on their own and usually got there by taking the streetcar. There were no team buses, no fences, and fans often stood in the deep outfield. My parents tried to come to the games. But my mom had taken a job in the Social Security office in downtown Chicago after my younger siblings started school, so she could really only make the weekend games. Same with my father.

Bill at bat for Gage Park High School at age 17, in #7 two years before it was worn by Mickey Mantle

After the war, sports broadcasting really started to expand, largely because baseball play-by-play came to television in 1947. That year, the first Major League Baseball contract, including the World Series, was signed for national television distribution. Two years later, the National Collegiate Athletic Association (NCAA) was created out of the Big 9 Conference Chicago office by Tug Wilson, Walter Byers, and Wayne Duke. Prior to the NCAA, the athletic conferences simply made agreements with each other to schedule and play games. About that same time (in 1949), the National Basketball Association (NBA) was formed when the Basketball Association of America (BAA) and the National Basketball League (NBL) merged. So now both college and professional basketball had new organizations to carry the sport into the future.

In April of 1950, I was granted a Rector Scholarship to DePauw University in Greencastle, Indiana. And it's a good thing, too, because I would not have been able to go to college without that scholarship. And my only alternate plan was to become the starting third baseman for the White Sox (my idea, not theirs). So, in 1950, I graduated from high school and went off to college.

Scorecard: 1940s

U.S. Population	132 million
President	Franklin D. Roosevelt Harry S. Truman
Major Events	U.S. Enters World War II (1941) Atomic Bombs dropped on Japan (1945) World War II Ends (1945) United Nations Formed (1945) Nuremberg Trials (1946) Marshall Plan (1948) Gandhi Assassinated (1948)
Most Popular Sport	Baseball
Sports Events	Olympics canceled 1940,1944 (WWII) Joe DiMaggio's 56-game hitting streak (1941) Ted Williams' .406 batting average (1941) Byron Nelson wins 11 Golf tournaments in a row (1945) Jackie Robinson joins Brooklyn Dodgers (1947) Joe Louis, heavyweight Boxing Champion (1937-1949)
Sports Additions	Basketball Association of America (BAA) Founded (1946) NASCAR Founded (1948) NCAA Founded (1949) National Basketball Association (NBA) Founded (1949)

New Technology	Penicillin (1940) 1st Commercial TV License WNBC (1941) Microwave Oven (1945) Polaroid Camera (1947) 1st Televised World Series (1947) Cable Television begins (1948) ABC TV begins (1948) Big Bang Theory (1948) Long-Play Phonographic Record (1948) 1st Non-Stop Flight Around the World (1949) Atomic Clock (1949)
Communications	Newspapers Radio Television
Average Baseball Ticket Price	$ 1.10

The Champions

MLB World Series

1940	Cincinnati Reds	(4-3)	v. Detroit Tigers
1941	New York Yankees	(4-1)	v. Brooklyn Dodgers
1942	St. Louis Cardinals	(4-1)	v. New York Yankees
1943	New York Yankees	(4-1)	v. St. Louis Cardinals
1944	St. Louis Cardinals	(4-2)	v. St. Louis Browns
1945	Detroit Tigers	(4-3)	v. Chicago Cubs
1946	St. Louis Cardinals	(4-3)	v. Boston Red Sox
1947	New York Yankees	(4-3)	v. Brooklyn Dodgers
1948	Cleveland Indians	(4-2)	v. Boston Braves
1949	New York Yankees	(4-1)	v. Brooklyn Dodgers

NFL Championship

1940	Chicago Bears	(73-0)	v. Washington Redskins
1941	Chicago Bears	(37-9)	v. New York Giants
1942	Washington Redskins	(14-6)	v. Chicago Bears
1943	Chicago Bears	(41-21)	v. Washington Redskins
1944	Green Bay Packers	(14-7)	v. New York Giants
1945	Cleveland Rams	(15-14)	v. Washington Redskins
1946	Chicago Bears	(24-14)	v. New York Giants
1947	Chicago Cardinals	(28-21)	v. Philadelphia Eagles
1948	Philadelphia Eagles	(7-0)	v. Chicago Cardinals
1949	Philadelphia Eagles	(14-0)	v. Los Angeles Rams

The Champions

NHL Stanley Cup

1940	New York Rangers	(4-2)	v. Toronto Maple Leafs
1941	Boston Bruins	(4-0)	v. Detroit Red Wings
1942	Toronto Maple Leafs	(4-3)	v. Detroit Red Wings
1943	Detroit Red Wings	(4-0)	v. Boston Bruins
1944	Montreal Canadiens	(4-0)	v. Chicago Blackhawks
1945	Toronto Maple Leafs	(4-3)	v. Detroit Red Wings
1946	Montreal Canadiens	(4-1)	v. Boston Bruins
1947	Toronto Maple Leafs	(4-2)	v. Montreal Canadiens
1948	Toronto Maple Leafs	(4-0)	v. Detroit Red Wings
1949	Toronto Maple Leafs	(4-0)	v. Detroit Red Wings

NBA Championship *

1940			
1941			
1942			
1943			
1944			
1945			
1946			
1947	Philadelphia Warriors	(4-1)	v. Chicago Stags
1948	Baltimore Bullets	(4-2)	v. Philadelphia Warriors
1949	Minneapolis Lakers	(4-2)	v. Washington Capitols

** Basketball Association of America (BAA) merged with National Basketball League (NBL) in 1949 to form the National Basketball Association (NBA).*

The Champions

NCAA College Football

1940	Minnesota
1941	Minnesota
1942	Ohio State
1943	Notre Dame
1944	Army
1945	Army
1946	Notre Dame
1947	Notre Dame
1948	Michigan
1949	Notre Dame

Heisman Trophy

1940	Tom Harmon	HB	Michigan
1941	Bruce Smith	HB	Minnesota
1942	Frank Sinkwich	HB	Georgia
1943	Angelo Bertelli	QB	Notre Dame
1944	Les Horvath	HB/QB	Ohio State
1945	Doc Blanchard	FB	Army
1946	Glenn Davis	HB	Army
1947	Johnny Lujack	QB	Notre Dame
1948	Doak Walker	HB	SMU
1949	Leon Hart	End	Notre Dame

The Champions

NCAA College World Series

Year	Champion	Record
1940		
1941		
1942		
1943		
1944		
1945		
1946		
1947	*California	(31-10)
1948	Southern California	(26-4)
1949	*Texas	(23-7)

** Indicates undefeated teams in College World Series play.*

NCAA College Basketball

Year	Champion	Record
1940	Indiana	(20-3)
1941	Wisconsin	(20-3)
1942	Stanford	(28-4)
1943	Wyoming	(31-2)
1944	Utah	(21-4)
1945	Oklahoma A&M	(27-4)
1946	Oklahoma A&M	(31-2)
1947	Holy Cross	(27-3)
1948	Kentucky	(36-3)
1949	Kentucky	(32-2)

Willie Mays

The 1950s

I graduated from Gage Park High School on the South Side of Chicago on June 25, 1950. That was also the day the Korean War started. North Korean armed forces crossed the 38th parallel and attacked South Korea. Two days later, President Truman, through the United Nations, committed our armed forces. With anti-communism on the rise after World War II, the President hoped to reunite the Korean Peninsula into a democratic stronghold as a counter to the People's Republic of China. Three years and two days later, on June 27, 1953, the war ended in a stalemate even though no formal peace treaty was ever signed. Technically, then, North and South Korea are still at war. Nearly 5 million people died during the conflict, including close to 54,000 Americans, and over 100,000 were wounded. It's often called the Forgotten War because it did not receive much attention from the American press. Television was still in its infancy.

During my four years in college, I played baseball and waited tables for my meals. My room cost $11 a month. In my junior year, some of the sororities decided to hire male waiters. And being no dummy, I applied to the Alpha Gamma Delta House and got the job. It was there that I met my future wife, Mickey. Both of us loved sports. It gave us a lot to talk about and, in no small way, sports bonded us. My degree was in economics, which prepared me for the many businesses I would later form (including ESPN). Being a very curious person who loved learning, I also had minors in history, geology, and geography.

After graduation I was commissioned an officer in the Air Force and sent to Eglin Air Force Base in the Florida panhandle, which, interestingly enough, had been the home of the Doolittle Raiders. At that time, the United States was the strongest military power in the world. We were also at the dawn of the Cold War – with the Soviet Union as the enemy – and Senator Joe McCarthy claiming that American society had also been infiltrated by communists. During those early years in the Air Force, it was easy to see that we were preparing and gearing up for a new rivalry that involved science, technology, politics, and propaganda. At Eglin Air Force Base, former German rocket scientist Wernher von Braun had an office in the Armament Center. And we received one of the first Remington Rand UNIVAC computers, which was so large it was delivered in an 18-wheeler – and part of the side of a massive hangar had to be removed to get it in. Even my father took advantage of new opportunities created by the Cold War build-up by taking a job with Thiokol Chemical (maker of rocket fuel) in Provo, Utah. He moved the whole family there, received a degree in Business (at the age of 60) from Weber State University, and eventually moved back to Chicago with a senior position in the banking business.

I continued to play baseball for the Air Force Armament team, on which we had a number of black players. But in Florida back then, only the military bases were desegregated, thanks to President Truman's 1948 executive order. Otherwise, Florida was very segregated, with separate drinking fountains and bathrooms for blacks and whites. But in 1954, the Supreme Court issued its *Brown v. Board of Education* decision, which ordered the desegregation of public schools. That led to a 1957 standoff in Little Rock, Arkansas, between Governor Orval Faubus and President Eisenhower to let nine black students into the all-white Little Rock Central High School. Faubus ordered in the State National Guard to prevent it, but Eisenhower countered by federalizing the guard. He also sent in the 101st Airborne Division – and that was that.

Once I got off active duty (and reported to the Reserves) in 1956, I was just not good enough to make it into professional baseball. So I was content to be a fan and, in the 1950s, there was a lot to revel in. For instance, on August 19, 1951, St. Louis Browns owner, Bill Veeck, sent a midget (Eddie Gaedel) up to the plate for one at bat. Detroit catcher Bob Swift told his pitcher (Bob

Cain), who was laughing, to "Keep it low." [Gaedel walked on four pitches and was taken out for a pinch runner.] Ted Williams spent part of two more seasons (1951 and 1952) as a pilot during the Korean War, and the New York Yankees were in eight of the ten World Series of the decade.

By the mid-1950s, television was growing rapidly – and I just happened to see Don Larsen pitch a perfect game against the Brooklyn Dodgers in the 1956 Series. A friend and I went over to the officer's club for lunch, where everybody was watching the game on a small black-and-white TV. By the sixth inning, word had gotten around the base and there was a standing-room crowd hanging on every pitch. In the bottom of the ninth, with the count 2-2 on Dale Mitchell, Larsen threw a pitch that looked high and outside to me. But umpire Babe Pinelli called it a strike. Game over. I can still see catcher Yogi Berra jumping into his pitcher's arms, while Mitchell tried in vain to protest the call.

While baseball was still "America's Pastime," other sports were up and coming. The NCAA started allowing one football game a week to be televised (starting with NBC). A slow emergence of the National Football League took place in the '50s, culminating in the "Greatest Game Ever Played," the 1958 championship between the New York Giants and Baltimore Colts (won by Baltimore in overtime). That game was televised nationally across the United States and portended the eventual impact on sports by the growing medium of television.

As Americans increasingly purchased TVs for their homes, the 1950s became the Golden Age of Television. Nearly everyone that had a set was parked in front of it in the evenings after work and school. And while big cities began televising baseball games, club owners resisted such coverage out of fear that fans would stop coming to the ballparks. However, most games were broadcast on the radio – even though, at first, the same argument was used to prevent radio coverage.

In 1954, Texas Instruments (with a company called IDEA) invented and sold The Regency TR-1. The "TR" stood for transistor radio. It weighed twelve ounces, resembled a pack of cigarettes, and was designed to fit into a man's shirt pocket. It sold for $49.99, was the first personal electronic device, and literally let people take live sports with them wherever they went. Soon, fans started bringing them to the ballpark so they could listen to the play-by-play. At one Dodgers game, announcer Vin Scully asked everybody at the park to say "Happy Birthday" to one of the umpires – and there were so many small radios present that 27,000 fans joined in.

It was clear that television was going to have a major impact on sports in the future. And I think it may have begun at the end of 1957 when the Brooklyn Dodgers and the New York Giants moved to the West Coast. Walter O'Malley (Dodger owner) clearly saw such a move as a great business opportunity, and he persuaded the Stoneham family (Giants owners) to move with him. This was a landmark in baseball history because before then, baseball had pretty much been limited to the Northeastern U.S. As a matter of fact, the only team west of the Mississippi was the St. Louis Cardinals – and the team farthest south was the Washington Senators (still north of the Mason-Dixon Line).

The 1950s has been called the "Golden Age of American Capitalism." We had a post-World War II booming economy that witnessed the rise of the middle class. Families had money to spend. They bought new cars and moved into houses in the suburbs. President Eisenhower pushed for the building of Interstate Highways, which propelled growth and prosperity. Nearly everybody had a job with opportunity for a career.

I went to work for Westinghouse as an advertising agent in 1957 at a salary of $95 a week. The company paid for me to go to Rutgers and get an MBA and when I came up with a new idea, I received a significant raise and promotion. That idea turned out to be so good that I left Westinghouse and formed my own advertising service company (AD AID, Inc). Our specialty was 24-hour order completion rather than the usual three or four weeks to several months. I went into the communities of East Orange and Newark, New Jersey – and hired virtually all women, especially stay-at-home moms. (There were only four men, including me, on the payroll.) We had over 100 women working every day and they rotated in and out based on their availability. Early on, I took an order from a small company that did not pay its bill. So I learned in a hurry to work with big companies like General Motors, General Foods, General Electric, S&H Green Stamps – and Westinghouse, which turned out to be one of my biggest customers. AD AID was a very successful business, but I was still determined to get involved in sports one way or another. And I knew I could eventually do it because there was so much innovation in technology that the opportunities seemed endless.

At my advertising company (AD AID), we employed almost all women

In the late '50s, we saw computers being developed, modems, credit cards, passenger jets, and lasers. We saw the evolution of major communications from local radio stations to national radio networks, to local television stations and national television networks. And they were all still using the AT&T phone lines.

Cable television also picked up in the early '50s in order to serve people who could not receive broadcasts over the air because of distance or mountains, etc. These small companies started buying Ditch Witches to bury cables to reach customers. No rights fees, nor any kind of permission, were received or even requested. They simply took network signals out of the air and rebroadcast them on their cables, which extended the reach of local stations. They paid nothing for programming. Eventually, the Federal Communications Commission (FCC) had to get involved to sort things out.

Generally, during the 1950s, there was a widespread sense of stability, peace, and contentment. It's a good thing, too, because all that was about to change.

First logos for the three major television networks

Scorecard: 1950s

U.S. Population	151 million
President	Harry S. Truman Dwight D. Eisenhower
Major Events	Korean War (1950-1953) Rock and Roll (1951) Cold War escalation (1953) Army - McCarthy hearings (1954) Brown v. Board of Education (1954) Civil Rights movement (1954) Castro takes power in Cuba (1959) Alaska and Hawaii become States (1959)
Most Popular Sport	Baseball
Sports Events	Bobby Thompson's Shot Heard 'Round the World (1951) Willie Mays' World Series Catch (1954) Brooklyn Dodgers win their only World Series (1955) Don Larsen's World Series Perfect Game (1956) Dodgers and Giants move to the West Coast (1957)
Sports Additions	*Sports Illustrated* 1st Published (1954) American Football League (AFL) formed (1959)
New Technology	Color TV (1951) UNIVAC Computer (1951) Ultra High Frequency (UHF) TV begins (1952)

	Polio Vaccine (1954) Atomic Submarine (1954) Artificial Intelligence (AI) introduced (1956) 1st Satellite launched, Sputnik (1957) NORAD Radar System (1958)
Communications	Newspapers Television Radio
Average Baseball Ticket Price	$ 2.00

The Champions

MLB World Series

1950	New York Yankees	(4-0)	v. Philadelphia Phillies
1951	New York Yankees	(4-2)	v. New York Giants
1952	New York Yankees	(4-3)	v. Brooklyn Dodgers
1953	New York Yankees	(4-2)	v. Brooklyn Dodgers
1954	New York Giants	(4-0)	v. Cleveland Indians
1955	Brooklyn Dodgers	(4-3)	v. New York Yankees
1956	New York Yankees	(4-3)	v. Brooklyn Dodgers
1957	Milwaukee Braves	(4-3)	v. New York Yankees
1958	New York Yankees	(4-3)	v. Milwaukee Braves
1959	Los Angeles Dodgers	(4-2)	v. Chicago White Sox

NFL Championship

1950	Cleveland Browns	(30-28)	v. Los Angeles Rams
1951	Los Angeles Rams	(24-17)	v. Cleveland Browns
1952	Detroit Lions	(17-7)	v. Cleveland Browns
1953	Detroit Lions	(17-16)	v. Cleveland Browns
1954	Cleveland Browns	(56-10)	v. Detroit Lions
1955	Cleveland Browns	(38-14)	v. Los Angeles Rams
1956	New York Giants	(47-7)	v. Chicago Bears
1957	Detroit Lions	(59-14)	v. Cleveland Browns
1958	Baltimore Colts	(23-17)	v. New York Giants
1959	Baltimore Colts	(31-16)	v. New York Giants

The Champions

NHL Stanley Cup

1950	Detroit Red Wings	(4-3)	v. New York Rangers
1951	Toronto Maple Leafs	(4-1)	v. Montreal Canadiens
1952	Detroit Red Wings	(4-0)	v. Montreal Canadiens
1953	Montreal Canadiens	(4-1)	v. Boston Bruins
1954	Detroit Red Wings	(4-3)	v. Montreal Canadiens
1955	Detroit Red Wings	(4-3)	v. Montreal Canadiens
1956	Montreal Canadiens	(4-1)	v. Detroit Red Wings
1957	Montreal Canadiens	(4-1)	v. Boston Bruins
1958	Montreal Canadiens	(4-2)	v. Boston Bruins
1959	Montreal Canadiens	(4-1)	v. Toronto Maple Leafs

NBA Championship

1950	Minneapolis Lakers	(4-2)	v. Syracuse Nationals
1951	Rochester Royals	(4-3)	v. New York Knicks
1952	Minneapolis Lakers	(4-3)	v. New York Knicks
1953	Minneapolis Lakers	(4-1)	v. New York Knicks
1954	Minneapolis Lakers	(4-3)	v. Syracuse Nationals
1955	Syracuse Nationals	(4-3)	v. Fort Wayne Pistons
1956	Philadelphia Warriors	(4-1)	v. Fort Wayne Pistons
1957	Boston Celtics	(4-3)	v. St. Louis Hawks
1958	St. Louis Hawks	(4-2)	v. Boston Celtics
1959	Boston Celtics	(4-0)	v. Minneapolis Lakers

The Champions

NCAA College Football

1950	Oklahoma
1951	Tennessee
1952	Michigan State
1953	Maryland
1954	UCLA / Ohio State
1955	Oklahoma
1956	Oklahoma
1957	Ohio State / Auburn
1958	LSU / Iowa
1959	Syracuse

Heisman Trophy

1950	Vic Janowicz	HB	Ohio State
1951	Dick Kazmaier	HB	Princeton
1952	Billy Vessels	HB	Oklahoma
1953	Johnny Lattner	HB	Notre Dame
1954	Alan Ameche	FB	Wisconsin
1955	Howard Cassady	HB	Ohio State
1956	Paul Hornung	QB	Notre Dame
1957	John David Crow	HB	Texas A&M
1958	Pete Dawkins	HB	Army
1959	Billy Cannon	HB	LSU

The Champions

NCAA College World Series

Year	Team	Record
1950	Texas	(27-6)
1951 *	Oklahoma	(19-9)
1952	Holy Cross	(21-3)
1953	Michigan	(21-9)
1954	Missouri	(22-4)
1955	Wake Forest	(29-7)
1956	Minnesota	(37-9)
1957 *	California	(35-10)
1958	Southern California	(29-3)
1959	Oklahoma State	(27-5)

** Indicates undefeated teams in College World Series play.*

NCAA College Basketball

Year	Team	Record
1950	CCNY	(24-5)
1951	Kentucky	(32-2)
1952	Kansas	(28-3)
1953	Indiana	(23-3)
1954	La Salle	(26-4)
1955	San Francisco	(28-1)
1956	San Francisco	(29-0)
1957	North Carolina	(32-0)
1958	Kentucky	(23-6)
1959	California	(25-4)

Muhammed Ali

THE 1960s

The new decade began with sad news for me, personally. My younger brother, Bob, who had joined the Navy after graduation from DePauw University, was killed in a training accident. He was an officer on the aircraft carrier USS Bonhomme Richard and was flying in the backseat of a two-seater jet when the plane went down. The Navy honor guard detail presented a flag to the family at the funeral. Afterward, my father went over to shake the lead officer's hand and say thank you. "Any time, sir," he responded. "Well, we certainly don't want to do this again," quipped my dad.

Nineteen sixty witnessed the first televised presidential debate in American history. John F. Kennedy defeated Richard M. Nixon by the narrowest public vote margin ever up to that point in time. Two years later, during the Cuban Missile Crisis, average citizens were building fallout shelters and children were doing drills to duck and cover under their schoolroom desks. At the time, the general public did not have most of the facts. We just saw the President frequently on television and heard a lot of short news reports and interruptions. But there were very few real-time facts. Most of the detail came out after Kennedy's blockade worked and the Soviet ships had turned around.

On my 30th birthday, a day before the Cuban Missile Crisis began, I left AD AID to pursue my dream of being a sports broadcaster. I sold my interest in the company to my two partners. In return, they paid my salary for three years, after which they would own full interest. [I'm proud to say that company stayed in business for fifty years.]

In *Broadcasting* magazine, I spotted an ad for a sportscaster from a radio station in Westerly, Rhode Island. I called, got an interview, and drove up to meet the station manager, Augie Cavalero. His first question was: "Did you bring a tape?"

"No. No tape," I replied.

"Where have you worked before?"

"Oh, I've never worked in radio before."

"What? Why are you here?"

"I want to break into the business," I explained. "And I want to be your sportscaster."

"You are the strangest job applicant I've ever had," he replied.

"Yeah, but I can do it, Augie."

"I like your attitude, kid. I tell you what I'm going to do. I'm opening a new station in Amherst, Massachusetts. It's small. It's a daytime station. You can be my sportscaster there. You'll prepare and deliver a morning sports show and go on the road to sell advertising time. If you'll move to Amherst by January 1 and help me with the FCC requirements to get WTTT on the air, I'll hire you at $150 a week."

"Done!" I said.

So I literally talked my way into the broadcasting business. Then I went home and talked to my wife. "We're going to do *what*?" was her first reaction. We had three small children (two sons and a daughter) at the time, but she was very patient and supportive. It was risky, of course, but I was a child of the Depression and World War II. Taking a chance didn't really bother me.

First photo in my new career as a sports broadcaster

My radio debut took place on April 1, 1963, at 7:45 in the morning. I just went on and started talking about sports, which was a blast. At WTTT, in addition to my show, I also broadcast University of Massachusetts football and basketball games. But in order to do that, I first had to receive permission from UMASS. So I met with the university's athletic director, Warren McGuirk, and first made a pitch to do football games. "Nobody will listen to it," he said. "But go ahead."

"Great!" I replied.

"Anything else?" he asked.

Surprised, I said: "Well, how about basketball?"

"Sure, why not."

It went that fast. Actually, I couldn't believe that he didn't ask for rights fees or some form of payment. But those things just weren't happening back then.

So now, because we were a daytime station, I had to make a deal with Augie to broadcast from a competing station in Northampton (WHMP) for night games. "You got football rights to do the games?" he asked.

"Yes," I said. "And basketball, too."

"How much is it going to cost us?"

"Nothing. We'll pay for it through advertising."

"Okay, let's do it," he said.

Before that, I had never called play-by-play in any sport. Actually, I had never even *seen* a college football game. But I did okay because my color analyst was the sports information director from UMASS, who provided all the statistics. One interesting fact was that UMASS not only finished the season undefeated, but also completed the season allowing only one touchdown, one point after, one field goal, and one safety (a total of 12 points).

I was driving to a Northampton game on November 22, 1963, when I heard on the radio that President Kennedy had been assassinated in Dallas. I bet I can take you to within ten feet of the spot on the highway where I heard the news. Everything just stopped – for me and everyone else all across the country. No football games, no school, no work. It was just the most terrible moment.

A couple of months later, I went to my station manager and asked permission to put together a small four-station (Northampton, Springfield, Greenfield, Pittsfield) nighttime network to cover UMASS basketball games. My next step was to call AT&T to work out a deal. "You'll have a dedicated network line and then we'll do local loops into each station," they told me. "It'll cost you a dollar per hour per mile."

I hired future Hall of Fame coach Johnny Orr and my buddy, Charlie Hill (who also had no radio experience), to be color men – and I did play-by-play for all the games. Then I had to get busy selling sponsorships. I went back to Westinghouse and S&H Green Stamps, secured them, and the Chrysler Plymouth Dealers of New England also signed on. One of my neighbors at the time was the advertising manager for Piels Beer. They had a very successful campaign called Bert and Harry, the animated Piels brothers. We got very creative with them and got about 50 Bert and Harry comments on audio tape. Then we put those together with common things that happened in a football game – like great catches, touchdowns, good running plays, and so on. Then after one of those plays during the game, I'd say, "Hey, Bert. Can you believe that catch Milt just made?" and the engineer working with us played the appropriate comment. We did that for the entire game and afterward, people were waiting for us at the bottom of the steps to meet Bert and Harry.

The animated Piels Brothers, Bert and Harry

So now I was a free-lance radio broadcaster and I owned my first network. A year later, we expanded from the western part of the state to an 11-station Massachusetts-wide network. It lasted for a couple of years and then I moved on. Today, the Redmen Network is viewed as a precursor to the New England Sports Network (NESN).

Johnny Orr (L) being interviewed by Charlie Hill (R) and me at halftime of a Redmen Network basketball broadcast

In January 1965, I left the radio station and moved into television by accepting a job to do weather and sports at the ABC affiliate in Springfield. But when I got there, I was informed

I would only be the weatherman and would be paid $10 a show, which didn't sit well with me. So, a few months later, when the sports director position at the NBC affiliate across town opened up, I applied and got the job.

And for the next nine years, I broadcast TV sports, hockey games, and an occasional football game.

About a month after I started that job, Muhammad Ali was in nearby Chicopee, Mass training for his second fight with Sonny Liston. The fight had been scheduled to be in Boston but had been moved to Lewiston, Maine, due to concerns about violence. (Malcolm X had been killed a few months earlier). I was invited to a sportswriter luncheon and a press conference for Ali and, because I was the new kid on the block, they designated me to ask the questions.

Beforehand, while I was sitting in the lobby of the hotel taking notes and preparing the questions, Ali walked over and sat down next to me. "How are you doing?" he asked. For the next thirty to forty-five minutes, we had a cordial and enjoyable conversation. For all his brashness on television, one-on-one, he came across to me as a perfectly regular guy and a gentleman. "Well, Bill, I have to go upstairs and change for the press conference. You're going to be asking the questions, right?"

"Right, Muhammad," I replied.

"Okay, good. See you then."

Pretty soon, reporters started assembling in the lobby for the press conference. Then suddenly, the room was abuzz and all attention shifted to the stairway where Ali appeared in all white - and I mean all white! He was wearing a white suit, white shirt, white tie, white shoes, white gloves – and started posing for pictures. Then he came down and said: "Okay, let's get under way. What do you want to know?" And then I was asking him my first question. He was only 23 years old at that stage in his career and our earlier conversation seemed to help him relax.

In the fall of '65, I began doing play-by-play for the Springfield Indians hockey team (a professional team playing in the American Hockey League). The owner was Eddie Shore, the NHL Hall of Fame defenseman for the Boston Bruins. And Eddie was one tough dude. The first time I met him was just prior to broadcasting one of the games. I brought a young engineer with me but Eddie didn't like something he said – so Eddie just stood up, leaned across the table and hit him square in the jaw. He pulled his punch somewhat and didn't really hurt the young man. But after that, it was all "yes, sir" and "no, sir" around "Mr. Shore."

During practices, I was allowed to go out on the ice and skate with the Indians. One day, I heard this authoritative, "Hey, Mister! Come over here!" I looked up and it was Eddie. So I went over and he said, "You're all right, but if you're going to do this, you really ought to learn how to skate." I'd been skating since age 5, but Eddie Shore gave me skating lessons on the spot. And later, at a morning practice, I heard that "Hey Mister!" again. This time he said, "All you do is skate and carry a stick. Do you know how to use that thing!"

"I haven't the faintest idea," I said.

"Well, come over here. I went over to one of the face-off circles where he had a bunch of pucks and he started backhanding shots to a mark on the boards. And he was within six inches of that mark on every shot."

"There, now you do that," he said.

Well, I tried a few, but I couldn't lift a puck backhanded if I practiced until Christmas.

"You're going to learn how to do this!" he said. "Keep shooting! Keep shooting!"

I continued broadcasting hockey in Springfield through the first year the Indians became a farm team for the Los Angeles Kings during the 1967 NHL expansion. Needless to say, Kings owner Jack Kent Cooke butted heads with Eddie several times. When the NHL union rep started talking with the players, Eddie Shore suspended his entire team. Of course, he finally relented, but he had clearly made his point.

In 1968, I was discharged from the Air Force Reserve as a captain. One week later, Dr. Martin Luther King, Jr. was assassinated. Shortly thereafter, it was Robert F. Kennedy. When the news reached us that Bobby had been shot in California, I was actually on the air. Normally, I only did a three-minute segment. However, NBC dropped all commercials from the air and the news presenters couldn't ad-lib the news. But they figured I could talk forever about sports. So the program director came in and said, "You're on until 11:30, Bill. Good luck." It was the first extended sports program I ever did – and I just winged it.

About that time, the owner of the AA baseball team in Pittsfield, Massachusetts (the Senators) had heard me announcing a football game on the radio and called to see if I'd be interested in calling play-by-play for their games. Of course, it had always been my dream to be a baseball announcer, so I said, "Sure." They paid me the princely sum of $25 a game. But after one season, I found that it wasn't what I thought it would be. I got bored with it and moved on. One highlight came when, during a game, I heard a knock at the door. I turned and it was Bob Feller, who asked if he could sit in for a few innings. "Of course, Mr. Feller," I replied. "Sit down."

Calling play-by-play for the Pittsfield Senators fulfilled my dream to be a baseball announcer

At the end of the decade, I was chosen to do the radio broadcast for the state high school hockey tournament at the Boston Arena. I thought it would be easy until they told me that they were going to play two games at a time. "What?" I asked. "How does that work?"

"First face off is at 7," came the reply. Turns out they had two teams play their first period, then they brought out two more teams to play their first period. Then the first two teams came out to play their second period. And that's how it went all night. The only time I got a break was when they stopped after every three periods to clean the ice. All the games were recorded and, afterward, the tapes were cut and spliced so they could broadcast the games whole. It was a real challenge to remember all the players – their names, stats, and what they had done in the previous period. I also had to do all the commercial breaks, for which I was given a restaurant menu from the sponsor and told to do two commercials during each period. "Wait a minute," I protested. "What do I say about this?"

"Well, you're the announcer!" I was told. "Figure it out!" I have to admit, after three or four periods in a row, the meals on that menus started to look pretty good. I also got to call play-by-play for the championship game in that tournament, which was played in front of 20,000 fans at the Boston Garden – home of the Bruins and Celtics.

The National Basketball Association really started to get going in the late 1960s, especially in Boston. Our station was given the opportunity to televise Boston Celtics playoff games, but first, we had to meet with the owner, president, and coach – Red Auerbach. When my boss and I went into his office, he was sitting behind his desk smoking his usual big cigar. "Let's talk about some rights fees," he said, right off the bat. But back then, there were no big bargaining agreements. No national contracts. No anything.

"What do you think we can get out of the local stations?" asked Auerbach.

"Oh, anywhere from $500 to $1,500, I'd guess."

"Okay," said Red. "That'll do. Make sure the checks for those rights are made out to Arnold E. Auerbach."

Of course, rights fees today are in the millions, sometimes billions of dollars.

The San Jose Sharks vs. the Anaheim Ducks, credit Elliot Lowe

Scorecard: 1960s

U.S. Population	179 million
President	Dwight D. Eisenhower John F. Kennedy Lyndon B. Johnson Richard M. Nixon
Major Events	Cuban Missile Crisis (1962) March on Washington (1963) Assassination of John F. Kennedy (1963) Vietnam War escalation (1963) Beatles visit America (1964) Civil Rights Act (1964, 1968) Medicare (1966) Assassination of MLK and RFK (1968) Woodstock (1969)
Most Popular Sport	Baseball
Sports Events	Ted Williams Retires (1960) 7th all time batting average (.344) 1st all time on base percentage (Babe Ruth second) Roger Maris hits 61 home runs (1961) Muhammad Ali wins heavyweight Boxing title (1964) Miracle Mets win World Series (1969)
Sports Additions	NFL Championship later designated Super Bowl I (1967) NHL Expansion (1967) American Basketball Association (ABA) founded (1967) NFL Expansion (1969)

New Technology	Laser (1960) Audio Cassettes (1962) Electronic Fuel Injection for cars (1966) Floppy Disk Drive (1967) Computer Mouse (1968) 1st Olympic Games Televised in color (1968) 1st U.S. Automatic Teller Machine (ATM) (1969) Artificial Heart (1969) Apollo 11 Moon Landing (1969)
Communications	Newspapers Television Radio
Average Baseball Ticket Price	$ 2.50

The Champions

MLB World Series

1960	Pittsburgh Pirates	(4-3)	v. New York Yankees
1961	New York Yankees	(4-1)	v. Cincinnati Reds
1962	New York Yankees	(4-3)	v. San Francisco Giants
1963	Los Angeles Dodgers	(4-0)	v. New York Yankees
1964	St. Louis Cardinals	(4-3)	v. New York Yankees
1965	Los Angeles Dodgers	(4-3)	v. Minnesota Twins
1966	Baltimore Orioles	(4-0)	v. Los Angeles Dodgers
1967	St. Louis Cardinals	(4-3)	v. Boston Red Sox
1968	Detroit Tigers	(4-3)	v. St. Louis Cardinals
1969	New York Mets	(4-1)	v. Baltimore Orioles

NFL Championship / Super Bowl

1960	Philadelphia Eagles	(17-13)	v. Green Bay Packers
1961	Green Bay Packers	(37-0)	v. New York Giants
1962	Green Bay Packers	(16-7)	v. New York Giants
1963	Chicago Bears	(14-10)	v. New York Giants
1964	Cleveland Browns	(27-0)	v. Baltimore Colts
1965	Green Bay Packers	(23-12)	v. Cleveland Browns
1966	Green Bay Packers	(34-27)	v. Dallas Cowboys
1967 *	Green Bay Packers	(35-10)	v. Kansas City Chiefs
1968 *	Green Bay Packers	(33-14)	v. Oakland Raiders
1969 *	New York Jets	(16-7)	v. Baltimore Colts

** 1967-1969 AFL-NFL World Championship Game, later called Super Bowl*

The Champions

NHL Stanley Cup

1960	Montreal Canadiens	(4-0)	v. Toronto Maple Leafs
1961	Chicago Blackhawks	(4-2)	v. Detroit Red Wings
1962	Toronto Maple Leafs	(4-2)	v. Chicago Blackhawks
1963	Toronto Maple Leafs	(4-1)	v. Detroit Red Wings
1964	Toronto Maple Leafs	(4-3)	v. Detroit Red Wings
1965	Montreal Canadiens	(4-3)	v. Chicago Blackhawks
1966	Montreal Canadiens	(4-2)	v. Detroit Red Wings
1967	Toronto Maple Leafs	(4-2)	v. Montreal Canadiens
1968	Montreal Canadiens	(4-0)	v. St. Louis Blues
1969	Montreal Canadiens	(4-0)	v. St. Louis Blues

NBA Championship

1960	Boston Celtics	(4-3)	v. St. Louis Hawks
1961	Boston Celtics	(4-1)	v. St. Louis Hawks
1962	Boston Celtics	(4-3)	v. Los Angeles Lakers
1963	Boston Celtics	(4-2)	v. Los Angeles Lakers
1964	Boston Celtics	(4-1)	v. San Francisco Warriors
1965	Boston Celtics	(4-1)	v. Los Angeles Lakers
1966	Boston Celtics	(4-3)	v. Los Angeles Lakers
1967	Philadelphia 76ers	(4-2)	v. San Francisco Warriors
1968	Boston Celtics	(4-2)	v. Los Angeles Lakers
1969	Boston Celtics	(4-3)	v. Los Angeles Lakers

The Champions

NCAA College Football

1960	Minnesota / Mississippi
1961	Alabama / Ohio State
1962	USC
1963	Texas
1964	Alabama / Arkansas / Notre Dame
1965	Michigan State / Alabama
1966	Notre Dame / Michigan State
1967	USC
1968	Ohio State
1969	Texas

Heisman Trophy

1960	Joe Bellino	HB	Navy
1961	Ernie Davis	HB/LB/FB	Syracuse
1962	Terry Baker	QB	Oregon State
1963	Roger Staubach	QB	Navy
1964	John Huarte	QB	Notre Dame
1965	Mike Garrett	HB	USC
1966	Steve Spurrier	QB	Florida
1967	Gary Beban	QB	UCLA
1968	O. J. Simpson	HB	USC
1969	Steve Owens	FB	Oklahoma

The Champions

NCAA College World Series

Year	Champion	Record
1960	Minnesota	(34-7-1)
1961 *	Southern California	(36-7)
1962	Michigan	(34-15)
1963	Southern California	(35-10)
1964	Minnesota	(31-12)
1965	Arizona State	(54-8)
1966	Ohio State	(27-6-1)
1967	Arizona State	(53-12)
1968 *	Southern California	(43-12-1)
1969	Arizona State	(56-11)

** Indicates undefeated teams in College World Series play.*

NCAA College Basketball

Year	Champion	Record
1960	Ohio State	(25-3)
1961	Cincinnati	(27-3)
1962	Cincinnati	(29-2)
1963	Loyola (IL)	(29-2)
1964	UCLA	(30-0)
1965	UCLA	(28-2)
1966	UTEP	(28-1)
1967	UCLA	(30-0)
1968	UCLA	(29-1)
1969	UCLA	(29-1)

Hank Aaron

The 1970s

Curt Flood played fifteen years in the major leagues with several teams. He won the Gold Glove seven seasons in a row as a centerfielder and earned two World Series rings with the St. Louis Cardinals. But when the Cards wanted to send him to the Phillies in December 1969, Flood refused to accept the trade or report to Philadelphia. It had been 100 years since the National League was founded, and baseball still operated under the Reserve Clause, which bound a player for life to the team that originally signed him. In other words, a player was the property of the team and had no say in trades. Despite being warned that he'd never get a job in baseball again, on January 16, 1970, Curt Flood filed a $1 million dollar lawsuit against Major League Baseball Commissioner Bowie Kuhn for violation of federal antitrust laws. He did it, in part, he said, because he hoped it would ultimately benefit the players.

Bombarded with hate mail and death threats, Flood refused to back down and took the suit all the way to the United States Supreme Court. On March 20, 1972, the court ruled 5-3 for Major League Baseball and against Flood. However, it also determined that while Flood had a right to be a free agent, baseball's reserve clause could only be removed by an act of Congress – and that the only way free agency could be achieved would be through collective bargaining. Because of pressure from their players, team owners agreed to binding arbitration through the MLB Players Union. And in 1975, Dodger pitcher Andy Messersmith became the first major leaguer to be declared a free agent. Almost immediately, player salaries sky-rocketed. Finally, in 1998, the U.S. Congress' Curt Flood Act did exactly what Flood had been asking for all along. The average baseball salary in '98 was nearly

$1.4 million dollars. In 1969, it was approximately $20,000. [Willie Mays was the highest paid that year at $135,000.] Curt Flood's courage not only influenced baseball, but hockey, as well. In 1972, the World Hockey Association (WHA), which had just started, challenged the NHL's reserve clause. When 67 NHL players signed with the WHA, the NHL tried to stop them, but got shot down in court. Afterward, salaries for professional hockey players rose dramatically.

In the early '70s, I was still with the NBC TV affiliate in Springfield as sports director and, later, news director. The WHA's New England Whalers began playing their games in the Boston Garden. But when the Bruins made the playoffs in 1973, the Whalers were told to find someplace else to play. So the Whalers moved to West Springfield temporarily, which is where I met team owner Howard Baldwin. Because the national networks had no interest in broadcasting the WHA playoff games, I offered to do them on the radio – and got the go-ahead. I persuaded Shaefer Beer to sponsor the broadcasts and then formed another small network with 4 or 5 radio stations in Massachusetts and Connecticut.

During the summer of 1974, the vice president of our TV station called and informed me that I'd need to get a hairpiece or he'd have to take me off the air. In those days, they would not hire female broadcasters (other than for the weather) and they would not allow bald male broadcasters. My hairline *was* receding and disappearing behind the shadows, but I thought this policy was really bothersome. So I prepared to move on. Just before I left, though, President Richard Nixon resigned (on August 9). That evening when we finished the news, I led a round-robin live discussion on Watergate with local and state government officials that lasted until 3 o'clock in the morning.

When their new arena was completed later in August (1975), the Whalers moved from West Springfield to Hartford, and I went with them as their new communications director. My job involved broadcasting, promotion – and advertising sales for the New England Whalers, which was an easy sell because everybody was excited to have them. I was paid the usual sales commission and I did so well that Howard Baldwin took away my commission, because he said I was making too much money.

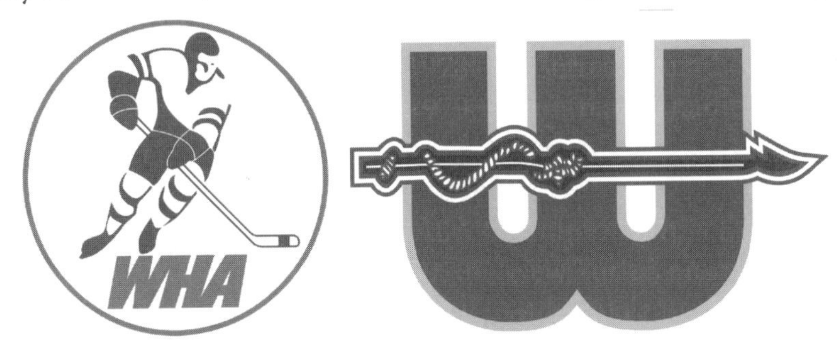

I went to work for the New England Whalers of the World Hockey Association after my television station boss said I would have to get a hairpiece

I went to work for the New England Whalers of the World Hockey Association, after my television station boss said I was too bald and would have to get a hairpiece.

In 1977, I had an idea to do a half-hour sports show, but the CBS network station in Hartford had no interest. There was, however, a religious station (WHCT-TV, Channel 18) that was having trouble filling program hours. So I talked to the onsite manager and asked if he could carve out the time. He agreed. So I worked for the Whalers during the day and, from 6:30 to 7:00 pm Monday through Friday, I produced and hosted the show I called *Sports Only*. Hilton Hotels was the sponsor and it became quite popular. Even Hartford resident Willie Pep (a Featherweight champion boxer of a bygone era) was a fan. One day he called and said that a bunch of his buddies were going to be in town and he wanted them all to be on my show. So, two days later, I had seven boxers on, including Pep, Jersey Joe Wolcott, Jake LaMotta, and Rocky Graziano. Just before we went on the air, I was trying to keep everybody quiet, so I could do the introductions when Willie shouted out, "Don't nobody ring no bells."

In 1978, former Detroit Red Wing hockey great Gordie Howe was the Whalers' leading scorer. He was not only 50 years old, but it had been six years since he'd been inducted into the NHL Hall of Fame. My son, Scott, became the arena announcer in Hartford. His position on the boards was between the two penalty boxes, and Howe was in the penalty box so often that he and Scott got to know each other very well. Then Howard Baldwin informed me that part of my new job was to be the executive director of Howe Enterprises, Gordie's private company (for which I received no additional compensation).

One of the great things about being involved in sports is that I got to personally meet legends like Joe Dimaggio (L) and Willie Mays (R)

I played on the Whaler's softball team that raised money for charity. In the summer of 1977, one of the charities announced that we were scheduled to play a game in West Hartford against a team of sports celebrities. I had no idea who might show up, but it turned out that broadcasting great Mel Allen was the public address announcer. Before the game started, I was at third base fielding ground balls from the first baseman when, out of the corner of my eye, I saw somebody walking up the third-base line right toward me. "Hi, I'm Joe DiMaggio," he said, holding out his hand. "I'm coaching third base." I shook his hand and could only manage to say, "Hello, Joe." That day, the clean-up hitter for the celebrity team was Willie Mays. When he came up to the plate in the first inning, I backed up and so did everybody else on the field. Willie started laughing in the batter's box and then he hit the first pitch over the left fielder's head – way over the left fielder's head. [Willie would be inducted into the Baseball Hall of Fame in 1979.]

On January 18, 1978, during a snow storm, the roof of the Hartford Civic Center collapsed from the weight of the snow. Fortunately, nobody was injured even though there had been a UConn basketball game there just a few hours earlier. Three weeks later, we experienced "The Great Northeast Snow Storm," as it later came to be known. Governor Ella Grasso closed the State down and asked President Carter for help. He sent the Army Corps of Engineers and 500 national guardsmen from Texas to help dig us out.

With their home arena destroyed, the Whalers went back to Springfield to play. And when they did not make the WHA playoffs that year, Howard Baldwin decided to clear out the executive office. So on Memorial Day weekend, 1978, I received a call from Colleen Howe (Gordie's wife) with news that the Whalers were firing me and that Howe Enterprises also no longer required my services. It was the first time I had ever been fired. All the other times I had quit because I wanted to do something else.

I don't think I spent a lot of time feeling sorry for myself. (Okay, maybe a little.) But I'd had an idea rolling around in the back of my head for several years and now it came to the front. There were legions of sports fans out there who would probably watch any kind of athletic competition, anytime, anywhere. The question was: How do we reach them? Then I thought: Okay, not being tied down to a job might provide an opportunity to do something big. I had gained plenty of experience over the years – not only in broadcasting baseball, football, basketball, and hockey, but also in building networks and advertising. Then

I thought to myself, *You're 45 years old. You're out of a job.* And I thought back to my grandfather first sparking my interest in sports by telling me stories about the White Sox beating the Cubs in the 1906 World Series and the magic of Tinker-to-Evers-to-Chance. *Chance*, I thought. *Why not take a chance? After all, I was still a member of the Silent Generation. I'd grown up during the Great Depression and World War II. What did I have to be afraid of?*

The best way to begin, I believed, was to start a sports network that would feed college and Whaler games to cable systems across the state. When that was successful, we could expand. I floated the idea by athletic directors at UConn and Wesleyan, who expressed interest. And even the Whalers told me that if I could pull it off, they were in. In fact, the athletic director at UConn, John Toner, and I began a serious discussion about televising the school's basketball, baseball, and soccer games and placing them on the cable systems in Connecticut. That interested some of the cable operators, but the Southern New England Telephone Company (SNET Co) told us that to make it happen, they would need at least a year to do site surveys and connect the lines.

Next, I went to a Connecticut cable conference on June 26, 1978, in Plainville, CT, and pitched the idea of this interstate cable network. At first, I was met with blank stares. But I pointed out that we were going to give them more programming, which would lead to more advertising, generally, and would open up local advertising across the state. "Well, we don't carry local advertising," said one station owner. "We just show whatever the networks have on. Besides, if we started doing that, I'd have to go out and hire an advertising sales guy!"

"Really?" I said incredulously. "Well, here's an idea: Hire an advertising sales guy, give him 10 percent and you keep 90 percent."

That was my brashest moment in the entire ESPN story. [At that time, there were only five operating cable companies in Connecticut. They were happy raking in seven or eight bucks from their subscribers for doing almost nothing and they simply didn't want to change.]

One person who did want to see some change was my friend, Ed Eagan, a Connecticut businessman who officed in the same building as the Whalers. He wanted to create a monthly cable program covering Connecticut sports. Rather than waiting around, Ed started videotaping local baseball games and hot air balloon races. When I told him about my dream, he was really excited, wanted to become involved, and became a partner.

Satcom 1, the first domestic satellite, made ESPN possible

At that June cable conference, one of the owners suggested we look into the possibility of using the new RCA satellite. In December 1975, RCA Americom had launched the first domestic communications satellite (Satcom 1) from the Kennedy Space Center in Florida. At first, the cable industry didn't want anything to do with it and RCA managed to market only two transponders. One went to HBO and the other to Ted Turner, who used it to make his TV station (WTCG) programing, including Atlanta Braves games, available to cable operators nationwide. [It became the Superstation and, as a result, the Braves became America's Team.] Turner was the first businessman to realize the amazing potential of using satellites to deliver programming to cable or broadcast television. At that time, the cable industry was a hardware-oriented business as opposed to a programming-oriented business. Receiving signals from a satellite would completely change the industry. The major factor was the footprint of RCA's Satcom 1, which was all of the United States, most of Canada, and part of Mexico. Suddenly, I realized that we could go beyond a statewide network and make our new company a nationwide network – almost instantly. Unlike Turner, who was restricted under the federal "passive common carrier" rule to distributing his Superstation programming unchanged, we would provide original content and have control over all aspects of the programming. And so, unfazed by all the negativity from the cable companies, we named our new enterprise, the Entertainment Sports Programing (ESP) Network, later shortened, of course, to ESPN. We incorporated on July 14, 1978.

I immediately called RCA and told them that I was thinking of using their satellite to do some things with the University of Connecticut. "Where are you in Connecticut?" asked the marketing rep. "I'll be up there tomorrow morning." It turned out that RCA was looking for someone to buy one of its satellite transponders and use it around the clock (for a cost of $34,167 per month). Turner's station signed off at 1:00 am (which was traditional for all over-the-air television stations) and HBO was only on five hours a night (at $1,250 per hour each night). We realized that if we took RCA's offer, we'd be the *first* network to broadcast a full 24 hours a day. "Whoa! Can you believe that? We could buy an entire 24 hour day for less than HBO paid per hour each night." So we took the 24-hour deal but were not required to begin paying until 90 days after the first use of the transponder. I committed ESPN even though I had no idea where I would get the approximately $1 million dollars needed – not to mention the money to set up nationwide operations on the ground. It was such a promising idea, however, that I felt confident the money could be found. By the way, shortly thereafter, *The Wall Street Journal* published a front-page featured article on Satcom 1 and, by the fall, all the RCA satellite transponders had been snapped up.

TBS and HBO were the first cable networks to make use of the satellite

In August, Scott and I were driving from Avon, Connecticut, to Ocean Grove, New Jersey, to attend my daughter Lynn's 16th birthday party. While stuck in a traffic jam on I-84 West in Waterbury, Connecticut, we started brainstorming about what our next steps needed to be and wrote them all down on a yellow legal pad. The first thing we determined was that we needed as much college football coverage as we could get, and not just from

Connecticut schools. So we had to call the NCAA, which only allowed three games to be televised each week. Their constant fear was that if they allowed more games to be televised, fans would not show up to the games, which was the same thing I'd heard when radio and television coverage for baseball was first proposed. But John Toner, the athletic director at UConn, didn't feel that way – and he was slated to become the next NCAA president. He suggested I meet with the chairman of the organization's TV committee, Bo Coppedge, which I did in September. Coppedge immediately invited me to make a presentation to the whole committee on October 15, 1978 (my 46th birthday). And that's when we got the ball rolling.

During that August car ride in the traffic jam, the idea of a nightly half-hour show with scores and updates came from the success of *Sports Only*, my local Hartford show. We called this version *Sports Central* (later changed, of course, to *SportsCenter*). Scott and I also talked about hiring on-air talent, production crews, programmers, advertising specialists, and all the other expertise we needed to build a successful business. We even sketched out the design for a headquarters building.

Of course, to make ESPN a reality, I knew we'd need a major investor. I had already taken the maximum $9,000 credit card cash advance and sold private shares to my family members who wanted to participate. So I hit the road and met with about a half dozen major investors to make my pitch, but was turned down again and again. Eventually, I spoke with Getty Oil Company, who didn't say no, but also didn't say yes.

I maxed out my credit card to get ESPN going

Next, I traveled to Denver (heart of the cable industry) to meet with cable companies. There were only about twenty of them in the country, but each owned sixty to a hundred franchises. At that time, they were referred to as MSOs (Multiple System Operators) and I met with as many of them as I could at the highest possible executive levels. I told them that we planned to deliver a 24-hour sports service to the cable industry at a cost of just a penny a day – and if they were looking for new programming, sports would fit the bill. I also pointed out that the satellites could deliver broadcast quality images just like the networks. [Most cable companies at the time did not.] Then I mentioned that they wouldn't have to work with the telephone companies or pay for any more lines. All they had to do was make a one-time investment of $5,000 for a receiver per franchise and they'd get all the channels they wanted.

Most of the MSOs didn't give us a very good response, though. In fact, I heard every reason in the book why ESPN wouldn't work: No one would invest in such a business; A channel focused on one topic was a terrible idea; There weren't enough sports to broadcast 24 hours a day; No one was going to watch sports that much; The satellites were going to fall out of the sky. Two executives literally laughed in my face. "Nobody is going to buy this!" they said. "It just isn't going to work."

The lone exception was United Cable. After mentioning what I thought was my brilliant "penny-a-day" proposal, Vice President Harvey Boyd said: "It'll never work at that price."

"Why don't you become the industry's first totally ad-supported network," suggested Bob Ball (also a vice president). "Somebody's eventually going to do it. Why not you?"

"A penny a day is just too expensive," said President Gene Schneider. "Bill, we're paying Ted Turner's Superstation ten cents a month – and all the upcoming new services want a nickel or a dime. And you're talking 30 cents a month. It just won't work on that basis."

After that bust of a road trip, I headed back to Connecticut and turned my attention to making ESPN ad-supported. I also went to visit John Toner at UConn to tell him about the satellite and its possibilities. He responded that he had just created a UConn Sports Package to be broadcast on cable television, which was to feature eleven of the university's varsity sports teams. When I suggested that we set up a demonstration package to televise his games using the satellite, John quickly agreed – and he announced the project on September 25, 1978, as a "joint development" between the UConn Athletic Department and "the Entertainment and Sports Programming Television (ESP-TV) Network of Plainville, Conn."

I was short on money and didn't want to start the 90-day payment clock with RCA, so I called a friend at the Madison Square Garden Network (which had just picked up a transponder) and arranged to rent their transponder for two games in one weekend. So, on November 18, 1978, we televised a UConn basketball game with *Athletes in Action*, a group of former basketball athletes that toured the country promoting good causes (such as community service). And that turned out to be the very first live event produced by ESPN. The next morning, we televised a soccer game between UConn and Rhode Island – and were off and running. Then, on January 9, 1979, we broadcast the first event using our own transponder. It was a basketball game between Rutgers and UConn that turned out to be an overtime thriller. Soon John Toner heard from alumni in both Alaska and Florida who had watched some of the events – and he was amazed that our idea had such reach. To be fair, though, it was hard for most people to grasp the real potential of one simple satellite signal being splashed all across North America.

UConn was a big part of our early success. In the spring of 1979, we televised a baseball game as a demonstration for the cable operators nationwide

On Valentine's Day, 1979, I was back in Kansas City visiting the NCAA, hosted by executive director Walter Byers. We had been talking for months, and this time he finally agreed to a deal. ESPN would broadcast 400-500 NCAA sporting events annually – at least one every day of the year. It was a two-year contract starting July 1, 1979. For exclusive rights, we would pay from $1,000 per live game for baseball, hockey, and minor sports – to $3,500 for basketball. For football, we could only broadcast tape-delayed games.

While I was still in the NCAA offices, I received a call from Getty Oil, informing me that they had decided to move forward. I was asked to fly to Los Angeles to meet with Stuart Evey, who was in charge of Getty's non-oil businesses. I had no idea what he was going to propose. But I was taken aback when he said: "We want an option for an 85-15 split and we'll give you all the money you need." I thought that offer was outrageous, but I kept my cool. When I started to say something, he interrupted me, "It's 85 or you can leave right now." At this point, we were out of money and had exhausted all possibilities for potential investors. Getty was our last option – and I had all these deals pending that would collapse without funding. A long time ago, somebody said to me that having a small part of something was a lot better than having 100 percent of nothing. And for me personally, it wasn't so much about the money as it was making ESPN a reality. Reluctantly, I said, "Well, if that's the way it has to be?" And Evey replied: "That's the way it has to be." So, on February 22, 1979, Getty made available an initial $20 million (which grew to $145 million) for us to launch the network with an option to purchase 85 percent of ESPN. The deal was immediately reported by *The Wall Street Journal*, *Sports Illustrated*, the *Sporting News*, *The New York Times*, and *Newsweek*.

Getty came through at the last minute with major funding for ESPN

In April 1979, we attended the annual convention of the National Cable Television Association (NCTA) in the Las Vegas Hilton Convention Center. We got there early and set up a 10' x 10' display booth at the end of a giant convention hallway. And we were lucky to get that one, which had a freight door next to it that opened to the loading dock.

After the first morning's welcome speeches, I was on a breakout panel discussion with six others, including Ted Turner, Bob Pittman, and John Coleman. But only five people showed up to listen. [Interestingly enough, we each founded a cable company of our own (ESPN 1979, CNN 1980, MTV 1981, and The Weather Channel 1982, respectively).] After that panel discussion, we were all walking to a restaurant when we stopped for a red light where there were more people waiting for the light to turn green than had been in our audience. So Ted Turner started preaching on that street corner about the future of the cable industry. I think it's also of interest to note that Coleman, Pittman, and I were all forced out of the companies we founded within a year (by the people in financial control).

ESPN (1979), CNN (1980), MTV (1981), The Weather Channel (1982)

The real fun at the convention started when our team (my sons, Scott and Glenn, Ed Eagan, and a couple of close friends) went downstairs and manned our booth. We had created a 5-minute video about sports and ran it continuously. We handed out hundreds of 8.5" by 11" information sheets – and our pitch was simple: "We have formed a 24-hour network. It'll be all sports. We have a deal with the NCAA. If you have a favorite team, we'll probably carry its games. Every night you'll see a half-hour sports show at 6:30 PM Eastern – the same time as the big three TV network newscasts. We want the local cable systems to carry us. And by the way, if you don't have a satellite dish to receive the signal, you're going to be way behind the times because *this is the future*."

Word started getting around and soon there was a big buzz on the convention floor. Seventy-five to 100 people crowded around us for the rest of the convention – listening and asking questions. There were cable operators, advertising agencies, and sponsors (such as Budweiser). One guy brought a female wrestling champion up and said he thought she would be a good feature on our network. We invited everyone to come up to our reception suite that evening – and it was packed, just absolutely overflowing. [A side note here: The next year's (1980) convention was held in Dallas, and we took up exhibit space for ninety 10' by 10' booths. We parked an 18-wheeler in the display hall with a stage set on the top of the truck. Our first interview was with Tom Landry, head coach of the Dallas Cowboys.]

A month after the convention (on May 25, 1979), Getty exercised its option – and now we had money with which to operate. So we began construction on a building in Bristol, Connecticut

– an industrial town known mostly for manufacturing clocks and machinery. In late 1979, we hired veteran broadcasters Lou Palmer, George Grande, and Jim Simpson, rookie broadcasters Chris Berman, Bob Ley, and Tom Mees, Dick Vitale (a fired NBA coach with no broadcasting experience), and dozens of other people (production crews, programmers, advertising experts, etc.) for ESPN. We also managed to lure the president of NBC Sports, Chet Simmons, into becoming our new president. I found it very interesting that, in April, he had been bad-mouthing ESPN – and on July 31, 1979, he came to work for us.

Chet's initial negative reaction to ESPN was par for the course because the big three networks were making a concerted effort to crush cable TV. The more people pushed cable, the more the networks did to keep it from getting into a competitive position. They even convinced *TV Guide* not to carry ESPN programming because, as they said, "*Real* TV networks have three letters, not four."

With our small band of believers (80 people), we launched ESPN on September 7, 1979 (at 7:00 PM) and became the cable industry's first totally ad-sponsored network – with clients like Budweiser, Hertz, *The Wall Street Journal*, Penn Tennis Balls, and the U.S Air Force Reserves. [Our $1.38 million contract with Budweiser was the largest single advertising contract ever signed in the cable industry (up to that point in time).]

Since that first day, ESPN has never signed off the air. [There would be no test patterns for us!] Many of the big metropolitan areas like New York, LA, and Chicago did not have much cable service. My parents, for instance, often had to drive to my brother's house in Peoria to watch a game they wanted to see and they would drive past motel after motel that advertised, "We Have HBO."

By the end of the year, my dad called me to tell me those same motels were now advertising, "We Have HBO and ESPN."

We were on our way when motels started advertising that they had ESPN

Scorecard: 1970s

U.S. Population	203 million
President	Richard M. Nixon Gerald R. Ford James (Jimmy) Carter
Major Events	Apollo 13 Returns Safely (1970) Pentagon Papers released (1971) Title IX Legislation – Women in College Sports (1972) Cable Deregulation (FCC) (1972) Munich Summer Olympics Hostage Crisis (1972) Roe v. Wade (1973) Watergate – Nixon Resigns (1974) United States Bicentennial (1976) Vietnam War / Cambodia Incursion / Ends (1976) Camp David Peace Accords (1978) Iran Hostage Crisis (1979)
Most Popular Sport	Baseball
Sports Events	Curt Flood challenges MLB Reserve Clause (1970) Miami Dolphins go undefeated (1972) Secretariat wins Triple Crown (1973) Aaron breaks Ruth's career Home Run record (1974) Ali beats Foreman, heavyweight Boxing Champ (1974) Nadia Comaneci Perfect 10 in Olympics (1976)
Sports Additions	AFL-NFL Merger (1970) Association for Intercollegiate Athletics for Women (AIAW) Founded (1971)

World Hockey Association (WHA) Founded (1972)
Designated Hitter introduced in Baseball (1973)
ABA Merger with NBA (1976)
24 hour Sports on Cable TV (1979)
WHA Folded (1979)

New Technology

Intel dynamic random-access memory (DRAM) chip (1970)
Microprocessor (1971)
Email (1971)
Home Box Office (HBO) 1st pay-TV network (1972)
Internet (1973)
1st Handheld Cellular Phone (1973)
Universal Product Code (UPC) (scan by optical laser) 1974
1st Personal Computer (PC) (1974)
RCA Satellite launched (1975)
Digital Camera (1975)
Concorde Supersonic Transport (SST) (1976)
1st Apple Computer (1976)
Voyager Space Probe (1977)
Sony Walkman portable cassette tape player (1979)
Video Home System (VHS) (1977)
Laserdisc (1978)
Quick and Dirty Disk Operating System (QDOS) (1978)
ESPN Launched (1979)

Communications

Television
Newspapers
Radio

Average Baseball Ticket Price

$ 3.30

The Champions

MLB World Series

1970	Baltimore Orioles	(4-1)	v. Cincinnati Reds
1971	Pittsburgh Pirates	(4-3)	v. Baltimore Orioles
1972	Oakland Athletics	(4-3)	v. Cincinnati Reds
1973	Oakland Athletics	(4-3)	v. New York Mets
1974	Oakland Athletics	(4-1)	v. Los Angeles Dodgers
1975	Cincinnati Reds	(4-3)	v. Boston Red Sox
1976	Cincinnati Reds	(4-0)	v. New York Yankees
1977	New York Yankees	(4-2)	v. Los Angeles Dodgers
1978	New York Yankees	(4-2)	v. Los Angeles Dodgers
1979	Pittsburgh Pirates	(4-3)	v. Baltimore Orioles

NFL Super Bowl

1970	Kansas City Chiefs	(23-7)	v. Minnesota Vikings
1971	Baltimore Colts	(16-13)	v. Dallas Cowboys
1972	Dallas Cowboys	(24-3)	v. Miami Dolphins
1973	Miami Dolphins	(14-7)	v. Washington Redskins
1974	Miami Dolphins	(24-7)	v. Minnesota Vikings
1975	Pittsburgh Steelers	(16-6)	v. Minnesota Vikings
1976	Pittsburgh Steelers	(21-17)	v. Dallas Cowboys
1977	Oakland Raiders	(32-14)	v. Minnesota Vikings
1978	Dallas Cowboys	(27-10)	v. Denver Broncos
1979	Pittsburgh Steelers	(35-31)	v. Dallas Cowboys

The Champions

NHL Stanley Cup

1970	Boston Bruins	(4-0)	v. St. Louis Blues
1971	Montreal Canadiens	(4-3)	v. Chicago Blackhawks
1972	Boston Bruins	(4-2)	v. New York Rangers
1973	Montreal Canadiens	(4-2)	v. Chicago Blackhawks
1974	Philadelphia Flyers	(4-2)	v. Boston Bruins
1975	Philadelphia Flyers	(4-2)	v. Buffalo Sabres
1976	Montreal Canadiens	(4-0)	v. Philadelphia Flyers
1977	Montreal Canadiens	(4-0)	v. Boston Bruins
1978	Montreal Canadiens	(4-2)	v. Boston Bruins
1979	Montreal Canadiens	(4-1)	v. New York Rangers

NBA Championship

1970	New York Knicks	(4-3)	v. Los Angeles Lakers
1971	Milwaukee Bucks	(4-0)	v. Baltimore Bullets
1972	Los Angeles Lakers	(4-1)	v. New York Knicks
1973	New York Knicks	(4-1)	v. Los Angeles Lakers
1974	Boston Celtics	(4-3)	v. Milwaukee Bucks
1975	Golden State Warriors	(4-0)	v. Washington Bullets
1976	Boston Celtics	(4-2)	v. Phoenix Suns
1977	Portland Trail Blazers	(4-2)	v. Philadelphia 76ers
1978	Washington Bullets	(4-3)	v. Seattle SuperSonics
1979	Seattle SuperSonics	(4-1)	v. Washington Bullets

The Champions

NCAA College Football

1970	Nebraska / Texas / Ohio State
1971	Nebraska
1972	USC
1973	Notre Dame / Alabama
1974	USC / Oklahoma
1975	Oklahoma
1976	Pittsburgh
1977	Notre Dame
1978	Alabama / USC
1979	Alabama

Heisman Trophy

1970	Jim Plunkett	QB	Stanford
1971	Pat Sullivan	QB	Auburn
1972	Johnny Rodgers	WR/RB	Nebraska
1973	John Cappellitti	RB	Penn State
1974	Archie Griffin	RB	Ohio State
1975	Archie Griffin	RB	Ohio State
1976	Tony Dorsett	RB	Pittsburgh
1977	Earl Campbell	RB	Texas
1978	Billy Sims	RB	Oklahoma
1979	Charles White	RB	USC

The Champions

NCAA College World Series

	Baseball *Men*	Softball *Women*
1970	Southern California (45-13)	
1971	Southern California (46-11)	
1972	Southern California (47-13-1)	
1973 *	Southern California (51-11)	
1974	Southern California (50-20)	
1975	Texas (59-6)	
1976	Arizona (56-17)	
1977	Arizona State (57-12)	
1978 *	Southern California (54-9)	** UCLA (3-0)
1979	Cal St. Fullerton (60-14-1)	** Texas Women's (1-0, 1-0)

**Indicates undefeated teams in College World Series play.*
*** AIAW Championship*

NCAA College Basketball

	Men	*Women*
1970	UCLA (28-2)	
1971	UCLA (29-1)	
1972	UCLA (30-0)	
1973	UCLA (30-0)	** Immaculata (59-52)
1974	NC State (30-1)	** Immaculata (68-53)
1975	UCLA (28-3)	** Delta St. (90-81)
1976	Indiana (32-0)	** Delta St. (69-64)
1977	Marquette (25-7)	** Delta St. (68-55)
1978	Kentucky (30-2)	** UCLA (90-74)
1979	Michigan State (26-6)	** Old Dominion (75-65)

*** AIAW Championship*

Hockey

The 1980s

My last day with ESPN was on December 31, 1980. I had founded the company and began with the titles, Chairman, CEO, and President. After we secured funding from Getty, however, Stuart Evey (Getty's designated point man) took over the CEO role. And after Chet Simmons became president, my role essentially changed to a nonactive chairman. The three of us started out working as a team, but that quickly changed. We were often at odds about how to move forward and, with time, our individual relationships became more contentious. Stu fired Ed Eagan, Scott quit, and I agreed to step aside and act as a consultant for three years. I really didn't have any anger about it – either then or now. If any one of us hadn't been there, ESPN would not have become what it is today.

Connectucut Magazine featured the launch of ESPN in Spetember 1979, highlighting the fierce attacks from "competitors"

In the three months before I left, a few things I was involved in are worth mentioning. The three major networks (ABC, NBC, CBS) were still working together to keep ESPN from growing into a competitor. For instance, they had a meeting with Nielsen (the TV ratings company) and informed them that the networks "owned" them and they could only report on their programs.

So Nielsen refused to rate ESPN or any other cable channel programs. Because they'd also put pressure on TV Guide, we printed our own television guides and sent out thousands of them. In response, TV Guide finally agreed to list us as *ESN*. [Remember, they told us that *real* TV networks only have three letters.] When the Federal Communications Commission (FCC) began an investigation into alleged anti-trust violations against the networks, I was asked to attend a meeting at the White House. This was in October 1980, a month before the national election. President Carter came in to meet us, and after I went through his receiving line, First Lady Rosslyn Carter walked over and just started chatting with me. She was very nice and very sincere. Of course, less than a month later, Jimmy Carter (despite leading in public opinion polls) was defeated by Ronald Reagan in a landslide.

In 1981, I moved to Tulsa, Oklahoma to work with Southern Satellite Systems at the request of its president, Ed Taylor. He felt that my work in founding ESPN could help him build his own business. Ed owned a new network, SPN (Satellite Programming Network), which broadcast old movies and a few other programs. While strategizing about how to grow SPN, I spent quite a bit of time in New York City working with some big advertising agencies. At the time, Southern Satellite Systems was selling Ted Turner's Superstation to cable operators for ten cents per subscriber per month. So Ed was on the leading edge of the burgeoning cable television industry. From him, I learned that, in addition to the video and accompanying audio component on each satellite, there was an outer band that could deliver an independent audio feed only. So Ed and I had the idea to create a cable radio network with several channels for music (classical, contemporary, county, etc.). We did, in fact, set up one channel for a trial run, but could not sell it to advertisers. Their argument was that nobody would listen to radio only because they would only want TV. But the concept was so new, we had no means of proving them wrong. So the idea faded away. Of course, it was resurrected twenty years later when Sirius Satellite Radio launched.

Meanwhile, at ESPN, Roger Werner joined the company in 1982 as vice president of finance, administration, and planning. Werner had been the lead consultant for McKinsey and Company when Getty engaged it to assess ESPN's future. His advice was simple. The company needed another $120 million and five years before it could turn a profit. And the only way to do that was to create a dual revenue stream. ESPN, Werner said, would have to start charging subscribers a significant fee in addition to increasing its ad-supported operations. [He takes credit for this idea in his book, but, if you remember, that was part of my initial presentation to the cable industry back in 1978.]

Earlier, in 1980, the company had implemented a nominal charge, which gave the cable companies the right to carry ESPN by paying $240 for five years. It was virtually nothing – kind of like a processing cost. But Werner, with the support of new CEO Bill Grimes, initiated affiliate fees paid by the cable operators according to the number of subscribers. Actually, at that time, ESPN didn't really know exactly how many individual households it reached. ESPN executives smartly phased in the new monthly fees so that cable operators weren't hurt financially. They went from six cents (1982) to ten cents (1983) to 13 cents (1984) and on up from there. But the cost really didn't matter because everybody wanted ESPN, which quickly became the largest cable network in the world. Moreover, with duel revenue streams, the company's financial value skyrocketed. [In 2017, the ESPN subscriber rate hit a peak of $9.06 per month. With nearly 100 million subscribers – well, you can do the math.]

On February 13, 1984, Texaco bought Getty Oil in an ugly hostile corporate takeover. An ESPN shareholder meeting was held in White Plains, New York, basically for me, my family, Ed Eagan, and a few people to whom we had given minor ownership percentages. The Texaco vice president running the meeting was brief and to the point. "We're examining all aspects of Getty," he said. "We are not in the television business, so we're going to sell ESPN. And I only have one question for all of you. Do you want to be getting dividends from Texaco for the rest of your lives or do you want a check at the closing?" Everybody said they wanted a check. "Okay," said the VP. And that was that - meeting over.

When word got out that ESPN was for sale, ABC had the strongest interest. But Ted Turner's financial adviser called me and expressed Ted's desire to bid and asked if I would put his idea forward with Getty. "We're sending you a check for $100,000 to make the offer to Texaco."

"Okay," I responded, "but I really don't think I can get anywhere with them."

"Well, if you try, you can cash the check no matter what happens." I agreed and did speak with Texaco, but got nowhere. For some reason, they would not even consider selling to Turner. It was the easiest $100,000 I ever made.

Texaco subsequently sold ESPN to ABC (on April 30, 1984) for $237.5 million. On June 25, 1984, I received a check for $3.4 million, and my family and Ed Eagan received their appropriate percentages.

What a game changer! The Supreme Court ruling against the NCAA opened the door for ESPN to explode

Two days later (June 27, 1984), one of the most momentous Supreme Court decisions affecting sports was handed down – *NCAA v. Board of Regents of the University of Oklahoma*. Since the late '70s, the NCAA had been sued from different directions by universities for the right to contract televised football games. In 1977, 63 schools joined to form the College Football Association (CFA), which had the networks pay $250,000 per game to any college that participated. After the CFA negotiated a major television deal, the NCAA threatened sanctions against all colleges in the CFA for all sports, not just football. In response, the Universities of Oklahoma and Georgia filed suit against the NCAA, asserting that it was in violation of the Sherman Anti-Trust Act. In the 7-2 decision, the Supreme Court ruled against the NCAA. That decision changed college sports broadcasting dramatically. And instantly, universities were negotiating their own deals with any network they chose. ESPN could now do football games live rather than taped delay. The number of football games on television rose, the rights fees paid to universities increased dramatically, and ESPN's growth took off like a hockey stick curve. As a result of that Court decision, football became the most popular sport in America (overtaking baseball for the first time).

Roughly concurrent with the breakout college football opportunities unleashed by the Supreme Court Decision, NCAA Women's sports rapidly gained television exposure as well. Title IX legislation enacted in 1972 mandated equal opportunity in sports for women. The Association for Intercollegiate Athletics for Women (AIAW) merged with the NCAA in 1982 and soon thereafter, Women's basketball, softball, and other championships became fixtures on ESPN and other local, regional and national cable television.

The NCAA Women's Final Four and Women's World Series are staples of the ESPN/NCAA long-term contracts to this day.

After receiving my check from Texaco, I moved to Naples, Florida, and bought a condo in a development that had a Jack Nicklaus championship golf course. Looking to take some time off, I played golf for twenty-one straight days and got bored silly. Then on Thanksgiving night, I received a phone call from my friend, Don Canham, Michigan's athletic director. "Bill, get up here. We're hiring you and we'll have a couple of meetings next week." Then he hung up. So, just like that, I was back in sports.

The Big Ten Conference had been suffering for years with regard to its broadcast exposure because the individual schools were stepping on each other's toes. Also, in the wake of the Supreme

Court decision, everybody was scrambling to get the best deals they could independent of the NCAA, which was in upheaval. When I arrived in Chicago for the conference meeting, Canham asked me what they should do. My immediate recommendation was to form a network just for the conference. They agreed, so we put together 94 stations for an over-the-air network from Maine to Hawaii. [This eventually grew into today's Big 10 Television Network.] We also created a merchandise business for which we produced trademark logo clothing for all the member schools – hats, shirts, pens, and other memorabilia. That doesn't seem like a big deal today, but in the mid-80s, it wasn't being done. I next went back down to Naples and, from the small office in my condo, became the Big Ten's official scheduler for basketball (1984-1986 seasons). I was also successful in putting together a four-year deal with ABC and a three-year, $33 million deal [Big Ten] with ESPN to broadcast Big Ten basketball games. In addition, I worked with ABC vice president Bob Iger to schedule football for the Big Ten. [Iger later became CEO of Disney]. The ESPN deal, incidentally, included the formation of Big Monday, which was a weekly double-header that included a Big East game at 7 o'clock and a Big Ten game at 9 o'clock.

I was involved in setting up the precursor to the Big Ten Network and then formed a new company called RCM Sports

In 1986, I started a new company, Rasmussen Communications Management (RCM), and entered into individual sports contracts with Illinois, Iowa, Michigan, Michigan State, and Purdue to help them with their basketball programs. Interestingly enough, unlike football, basketball had never been regulated – simply because the big three networks never thought the sport was a big deal. The schools I contracted with never had any kind of television coverage at all. When I got to Iowa, for instance, the stations were charging the university to televise games. "That's not the way it works," I told Bump Elliott, the school's athletic director. "They pay you."

"Really?" Bump replied. "You can do that?"

"Sure can," I said. Then we began work on the Hawkeye Television Network and let all the big city television stations bid. One station owner wrote me a letter with a $250,000 check enclosed. "Make us the Hawkeye Network station in our market and you can cash this check." I sent it right back and informed him that his station was out of the running. I also negotiated and sold advertising for all the stations, which was easy because everybody associated with the corn industry were big Hawkeye fans. Iowa went from spending $200,000 per year to bringing in $1.3 million (for the 1987-1988 season).

With RCM Sports, I also got into the production business. The Big Ten gave us a contract and paid the production costs for games that we uplinked from our brand new headquarters in Champagne, IL. We scheduled, produced, and delivered basketball games on television throughout the Midwest. Our broadcasters worked freelance – including some big names like Chris Schenkel and Jim Simpson. We also produced both football and basketball coaches shows, and when ABC or CBS came in, we provided production facilities and uplinks. We had around thirty full-time employees, five of them worked in advertising. Budweiser, Monsanto, and Allstate were three of our largest clients.

Around that time, I suggested that the Big Ten put together a post-season basketball tournament. I provided chart analysis to show them that they'd make a lot of money. Although I was unable to convince them to launch a post season tournament, we *did* put we did put together a four-team (Louisville, Kentucky, Notre Dame, Indiana) invitational at the Hoosier Dome in Indianapolis. We allocated 50,000 tickets (12,500 to each school) and sold out immediately. [Louisville won, by the way.] I never could convince the Big Ten to do a post-season tournament, mostly because Bobby Knight was against it. [They finally started one in 1998.]

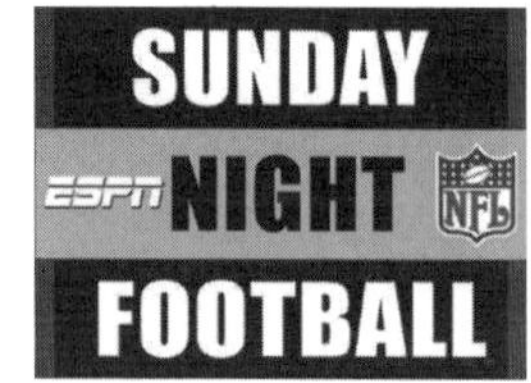

ESPN launched the first international sports network (1989) and secured Sunday Night Football (1987)

It was right around then that an article appeared in TV Guide noting that ESPN posted a $100 million profit in 1989 – and that same year ABC (who bought ESPN five years earlier) lost $8 million. Overall, the decade of the 1980s saw an explosion of sports coverage on television. More specifically, ESPN began distributing its programming internationally (1983) and launched its first international network in Central and South America (ESPN International, 1989). Also in 1989, the company signed a four-year agreement to broadcast Major League Baseball for the first time (starting in 1990). ESPN also became the first cable network to televise regular-season NFL games with "ESPN's Sunday Night Football" in 1987. And it went on to redefine pre- and post-game analysis with shows like "NFL Countdown" and "NFL Primetime."

Spurred by football, there were now more fans and more people who wanted to go to the ballpark. So bigger arenas had to be built and the price of tickets went up. From the 1940s to the 1980s, some team owners were afraid to let their team's games be broadcast. But thanks to ESPN, in great part, they admitted that they had been wrong all along. For me, personally, that was as big a deal as the Fall of the Berlin Wall, which also came down in 1989.

Chris Berman was a trend setter from day 1. His contribution to the ESPN fan's experience is monumental. Boomer began hosting the Monday Night NFL Countdown show in 1989, long before ESPN first televised Monday Night Football in 2006

Scorecard: 1980s

U.S. Population	226 million
President	James (Jimmy) Carter Ronald Reagan George H. W. Bush
Major Events	24 hour News on Cable TV (1980) Iran Hostage Crisis (1979-1981) HIV / AIDS Epidemic (1981) 1st Female on Supreme Court, Sandra Day O'Connor (1981) Attempted Assassination of Ronald Reagan (1981) Space Shuttle Challenger Explosion (1986) Chernobyl Nuclear Disaster (1986) Reagan and Gorbachev sign the INF Treaty (1987) Exxon Valdez Oil Spill (1989) Fall of the Berlin Wall (1989)
Most Popular Sport	Football
Sports Events	USA Olympic "Miracle on Ice" Hockey team v. USSR 1980 NC State Shocks Houston in NCAA Basketball final (1983) Pete Rose breaks Ty Cobb Career Hits record: 4,192 (1985) Jack Nicklaus wins 6th Masters (1986) Wayne Gretzky traded from Edmonton to LA (1988) Pete Rose banned from Baseball (1989)

Sports Additions	NCAA Women's Championships begin (1982) Supreme Court Decision, NCAA v. Board of Regents of the Univ. of Oklahoma (1984) ABC buys ESPN (1984)
New Technology	1st Space Shuttle launch (1981) IBM Personal Computer with MS-DOS (1981) At-home Banking begins (1981) CNN (1980) MTV (1981) Weather Channel (1982) Compact Disc (CD) (1982) Camcorder (1983) DNA Fingerprinting (1984) Microsoft Windows operating system (1985) America Online (AOL) (1985) Jumbotron (1985)
Communications	Television Radio Newspapers
Average Baseball Ticket Price	$6.00

The Champions

MLB World Series

1980	Philadelphia Phillies	(4-2)	v. Kansas City Royals
1981	Los Angeles Dodgers	(4-2)	v. New York Yankees
1982	St. Louis Cardinals	(4-3)	v. Milwaukee Brewers
1983	Baltimore Orioles	(4-1)	v. Philadelphia Phillies
1984	Detroit Tigers	(4-1)	v. San Diego Padres
1985	Kansas City Royals	(4-3)	v. St. Louis Cardinals
1986	New York Mets	(4-3)	v. Boston Red Sox
1987	Minnesota Twins	(4-3)	v. St. Louis Cardinals
1988	Los Angeles Dodgers	(4-1)	v. Oakland Athletics
1989	Oakland Athletics	(4-0)	v. San Francisco Giants

NFL Super Bowl

1980	Pittsburgh Steelers	(31-1)	v. Los Angeles Rams
1981	Oakland Raiders	(27-10)	v. Philadelphia Eagles
1982	San Francisco 49ers	(26-21)	v. Cincinnati Bengals
1983	Washington Redskins	(27-17)	v. Miami Dolphins
1984	Los Angeles Raiders	(38-9)	v. Washington Redskins
1985	San Francisco 49ers	(38-16)	v. Miami Dolphins
1986	Chicago Bears	(46-10)	v. New England Patriots
1987	New York Giants	(39-20)	v. Denver Broncos
1988	Washington Redskins	(42-10)	v. Denver Broncos
1989	San Francisco 49ers	(20-16)	v. Cincinnati Bengals

The Champions

NHL Stanley Cup

1980	New York Islanders	(4-2)	v. Philadelphia Flyers
1981	New York Islanders	(4-1)	v. Minnesota North Stars
1982	New York Islanders	(4-0)	v. Vancouver Canucks
1983	New York Islanders	(4-0)	v. Edmonton Oilers
1984	Edmonton Oilers	(4-1)	v. New York Islanders
1985	Edmonton Oilers	(4-1)	v. Philadelphia Flyers
1986	Montreal Canadiens	(4-1)	v. Calgary Flames
1987	Edmonton Oilers	(4-3)	v. Philadelphia Flyers
1988	Edmonton Oilers	(4-0)	v. Boston Bruins
1989	Calgary Flames	(4-2)	v. Montreal Canadiens

NBA Championship

1980	Los Angeles Lakers	(4-2)	v. Philadelphia 76ers
1981	Boston Celtics	(4-2)	v. Houston Rockets
1982	Los Angeles Lakers	(4-2)	v. Philadelphia 76ers
1983	Philadelphia 76ers	(4-0)	v. Los Angeles Lakers
1984	Boston Celtics	(4-3)	v. Los Angeles Lakers
1985	Los Angeles Lakers	(4-2)	v. Boston Celtics
1986	Boston Celtics	(4-2)	v. Houston Rockets
1987	Los Angeles Lakers	(4-2)	v. Boston Celtics
1988	Los Angeles Lakers	(4-3)	v. Detroit Pistons
1989	Detroit Pistons	(4-0)	v. Los Angeles Lakers

THE CHAMPIONS

NCAA College Football

1980	Georgia
1981	Clemson
1982	Penn State
1983	Miami (Fla)
1984	Brigham Young
1985	Oklahoma
1986	Penn State
1987	Miami (Fla)
1988	Notre Dame
1989	Miami (Fla)

Heisman Trophy

1980	George Rogers	RB	South Carolina
1981	Marcus Allen	RB	USC
1982	Herschel Walker	RB	Georgia
1983	Mike Rozier	RB	Nebraska
1984	Doug Flutie	QB	Boston College
1985	Bo Jackson	RB	Auburn
1986	Vinnie Testaverde	QB	Miami
1987	Tim Brown	WR	Notre Dame
1988	Barry Sanders	RB	Oklahoma State
1989	Andre Ware	QB	Houston

The Champions

NCAA College World Series

	Baseball Men	Softball Women
1980	Arizona (45-21-1)	** Utah St. (1-0)
1981	Arizona State (55-13)	** Utah St. (1-6, 4-3)
1982 *	Miami (Fla.) (55-17-1)	* UCLA (33-7-2)
1983 *	Texas (66-14)	Texas A&M (41-11)
1984	Cal St. Fullerton (66-20)	UCLA (45-6-1)
1985	Miami (Fla.) (64-16)	UCLA (41-9)
1986	Arizona (49-19)	* Cal State Fullerton (57-9-1)
1987	Stanford (53-17)	Texas A&M (56-8)
1988	Stanford (46-23)	UCLA (53-8)
1989	Wichita State (68-16)	* UCLA (48-4)

**Indicates undefeated teams in College World Series play.*

***AIAW Championship*

NCAA College Basketball

	Men	Women
1980	Louisville (33-3)	** Old Dominion (68-53)
1981	Indiana (26-9)	** Louisiana Tech (79-59)
1982	North Carolina (32-2)	Louisiana Tech (35-1)
1983	NC State (26-10)	Southern California (31-2)
1984	Georgetown (34-3)	Southern California (29-4)
1985	Villanova (25-10)	Old Dominion (31-3)
1986	Louisville (32-7)	Texas (34-0)
1987	Indiana (30-4)	Tennessee (28-6)
1988	Kansas (27-11)	Louisiana Tech (32-2)
1989	Michigan (30-7)	Tennessee (35-2)

***AIAW Championship*

Hockey

The 1990s

On September 19, 1994, *Sports Illustrated* published a 40th-anniversary issue, which celebrated the forty people "who had most dramatically elevated and altered the games we play and watch" during those four decades." Muhammad Ali was #1. I was #29 (twelve spots behind Secretariat). A banquet was held in New York and most of the forty selected showed up. I didn't see Secretariat there, but I did run into Muhammad Ali, who immediately recognized me from our press conference twenty-five years earlier.

Twenty-five years after I met Muhammad Ali just before the second Liston fight, I saw him again at the Sports Illustrated 40th anniversary celebration. We had a great time catching up

"Hi again!" he said. "Then he pointed and said, 'Is this your wife?'"

"Sure is," I replied.

"Well, she's the boss, Bill. Pay attention to her."

I also met legendary UCLA basketball coach John Wooden. "Oh, yeah, ESPN," he said. "That's the worst thing that ever happened to college sports." I think it would have been more accurate if he'd said that ESPN was the worst thing that ever happened to UCLA *recruiting*, because the Bruins no longer had a monopoly on the nation's attention. Every team was now on television.

By 1990, RCM Sports wrapped up its contracts. My next venture was with a company that manufactured integrated home automation systems that, from a distance, electronically controlled a home's energy, security, lights, heating, air conditioning, and so on. From 1990 to 1993, I was President and Chairman of IntelliNet and, during those years, the business grew and flourished. It did so well, in fact, that we decided to sponsor a tournament on the Senior PGA Tour. At the time, Naples had the oldest continuously sponsored tournament, which Aetna had supported for years. When they bowed out after the 1993 tournament, we met with the PGA, offered a bid of $500,000, and were awarded the sponsorship, which we kept for three years. Played in February of every year, the IntelliNet Challenge really elevated our business profile, not to mention the fact that I got to play golf with Lee Trevino, Gary Player, Bob Murphy, Homero Blancas, Bob Charles, and other SeniorPGA pros.

As President and Chairman of IntelliNet, I helped secure a sponsorship on the PGA Senior Tour

One month after our first IntelliNet Challenge, I was invited to play at Augusta National Golf Club, home of the Masters. I played at golf courses from San Diego to Maine and places in between, but every golfer aspires to play at Augusta and, after just a few holes, I could see why. We were there just a few weeks before the Masters was played and the place was immaculate and absolutely beautiful. I really believe the beauty of Augusta lifted my game because I had a 40 on the front nine and a 43 on the back, but parred all three holes at Amen Corner (holes 11, 12, and 13) to finish with an 83. That evening, before going to sleep in the historic Eisenhower cabin, I reflected on Amen Corner and my entire game and couldn't have been happier.

Only one thing could top that amazing feeling. The highlight of my time in Naples was when I was invited to play in a foursome with President George H.W. Bush. On the first hole, when it was his turn to putt, he looked up, waiting for someone to give him a three footer. I said, "Presidential privilege only goes so far. Putt!"

He stepped back, laughed, and replied, "Game on!" Then he made his putt. We all relaxed and had a great time.

The IntelliNet idea was a good one, but, unfortunately, our technology was hard-wired and predated wireless technology. When wireless became the obvious choice, our partners were not willing to invest in the new technology. So the company had to drop sponsorship of the golf tournament and eventually faded away. But I stayed on as the tournament director and was successful in recruiting the LG Corporation to fill the sponsorship void.

The Internet not only changed the course of industries and interactions between sellers and buyers, it also revolutionized sports. Broadcasting flourished with radio and television. But when the Internet was fully augmented, it dramatically increased the number of options for fans to enjoy sports. Coverage would become available almost everywhere, all the time. For the most popular sports, rights fees would skyrocket. The less popular sports would gain increased visibility, which translated into more sponsors, higher player salaries, and increased rights fees, as well. Actually, the Internet would increase viewership for all sports all around the world. More people showed up at games – and instant fan interaction would take place during and after games. The World Wide Web would create an unbelievable transformation in almost everything people did around the world, especially sports.

In mid-1996, another new idea emerged. "Wouldn't it be great if we could build a new kind of golf venue?" I wondered. Envision building a multi-deck 12,000-seat grandstand wrapped around the 18th green of a championship golf course. It would look like a ballpark and would include luxury skyboxes, condominiums and would

Stadium Naples™ at the 18th hole

accommodate thousands of general admission ticket holders with spectacular views of the closing holes. In addition to the stadium condos, I thought that this top tier course could offer a limited number of luxury home building lots for sale. It would be a perfect venue for professional golf tournaments of both the regular and senior PGA tours, the Ryder Cup, and any made-for-TV event. Corporations could also have their own outings there, and, we thought, it could be a permanent home for the Tour's Qualifying [Q] School.

Stadium Naples™ grand entrance

In the business proposal for Stadium Naples™, I figured we'd need to buy about two square miles of land in the northeast corner of the City of Naples. And, of course, we would need architects (of which there were plenty of in our area) to draw up the plans. The total project estimate was about $100 million. The next step was to engage a great developer – and I chose Bob Hardy, who had built several first-class golf clubs in Florida. For financing, Bob brought on a hedge fund manager named David Mobley, who was producing an unbelievable annual return for his clients. A nice guy with a great personality, David assured all of us that he could raise enough money for the project without any problem. Contracts were drawn up and finalized. After receiving approval from the County, we went looking for a golf course designer. We spoke with representatives of Gary Player, Arnold Palmer, and Jack Nicklaus. But before we could choose one, or even break ground, everything fell apart in early 2000.

Barron's, a financial magazine, published a major article on David Mobley and his hedge fund. On the front page, he was pictured sitting on a beach under an umbrella in a sportscoat and bare feet, claimed that he had a $450 million hedge fund producing unbelievable results and that he was looking for more investors. But that article resulted in Mobley being exposed as a fraud. It turned out that his "unbelievable" returns had been completely false. The Securities and Exchange Commission (SEC) got involved, determined he had fabricated monthly statements and funneled millions of his investor's money to himself and his shell companies. It was all a Ponzi scheme. The story was on the front page of the *Naples Daily News* every day for weeks, months, and years. A special prosecutor from Miami conducted a detailed investigation. [You know how they can be. It turned out that the prosecutor was very aggressive, very difficult, and egotistical. He got carried away with his power and treated all 10 of us as bad guys and criminals. The truth was that the *only* criminal involved was David Mobley.]

I had a scare when I was in South Carolina. My attorney called and said, "This guy (the special prosecutor) believes that you've got some information he needs, so he's planning to have you arrested and held in jail until he can arrive to take your statement. Get out right now! He's on the way." So I immediately returned to Naples and the two of us went to the courtroom of the judge who had authorized the arrest warrant. There were just three of us in the courtroom. The judge got on the phone with the special prosecutor, who quickly said, "I've arranged for the arrest warrant to be served and I'll have him shortly."

"What are you talking about?" asked the judge, "He's standing right here in front of me." There was a long silence and then the judge finally said, "I don't want to hear any more about this from you." And she hung up. I had a very competent attorney.

The investigations revealed that Mobley had an undisclosed criminal past in Toledo, Ohio and had been working his scam in Naples for seven years. A federal grand jury indicted him on twenty counts of fraud and tax evasion. As part of the proceedings, along with the eight others, I testified without any qualms since I had nothing to hide. Mobley pled guilty and was sentenced to 17 and a half years in prison and ordered to pay $77 million in restitution. The investigations also found that *only* Mobley had acted with criminal intent. This cleared me of any suspicion, however, everybody involved lost a lot of money.

There was some very negative press for several years. The local newspaper figured out early on they could keep selling papers by putting my name in the headline, forcing me to file a lawsuit against them. In their 2005 story reporting the end of the lawsuit, they defamed me *again*, this time accusing me of being convicted, which was not true. To avoid another lawsuit, the editor published a retraction. And when it was discovered hidden deep inside the paper, they had to publish it *again*. This time, "A correction and an apology" states that their coverage defamed me over the span of 7 years in the hundreds of stories they published about Mobley. "Our record of accuracy, however, ended last week when we published a story about Rasmussen," admitting their guilt. Instead of burying it, the editor published the article on the *front* page of the second section in the Sunday, January 1, 2006 edition, stating, "He wasn't convicted of anything." It was egg on the face of the editor who was caught in the lie and admitted, "We made a mistake and we are sorry."

That ended a really long and difficult stretch that not only impacted my professional life, but my family and friends too. It was tough being targeted day after day for over seven years. To this very day, these unfounded attacks bother me. Talk about Fake News - I've experienced it first hand.

Ted Williams threw out the first pitch in the 1999 All-Star Game at Fenway Park. When he arrived on a golf cart, the Red Sox fans gave him a rousing ovation and welcome back. After the cart driver took him on a lap around the field, he threw out the game ball from the pitcher's mound. And then all the All-Star players crowded around Ted to shake his hand, chat with him, and just be near him. The players lingered as long as they could and everyone could see that Ted was visibly moved. With tears streaming down his face, he told Carlton Fisk that it was one of the greatest moments of his life. For me, this was the end of an era where baseball players were heroes on the ballfield and the battlefield. Imagine what his stats would look like had he not missed 3 full seasons (WWII) and almost all of 2 other seasons (Korea)? He holds the on base percentage record to this day!

The last full decade of the twentieth century witnessed a sports television boom. Countless new contracts were signed by virtually every sports team and organization. One good example is the CBS agreement for exclusive rights to televise the NCAA basketball tournament for all games after the first round. The NCAA was paid $166.5 million over three years by CBS.

The incredible expansion by ESPN in the 1990s included four television networks, a radio network, a sports website and a magazine [not all of them exist today]:

ESPN Radio

ESPN2

ESPN *Classic*

ESPNEWS

ESPN *The Magazine*

ESPN Now

ESPN Extra

ESPN was acquired by Disney (through its purchase of ABC) in 1996, and the company's accomplishments at the end of the century were remarkable. It had launched a second channel, ESPN 2 (1993) and everybody said, "Are you serious? Twenty-four more hours of sports?" Well, I guess so because ESPN Classic launched in 1995 and then ESPNEWS in 1996. *ESPN The Magazine* started in 1998 and eventually passed *Sports Illustrated* in circulation. In 1999, the company launched two more short-lived digital streaming channels (ESPN Now and ESPN Extra). The new ESPN Internet Group set an online sports record with 8.2 million users. ESPN was now the largest sports television network in America and was in 77 million homes. ESPN Radio launched on January 1, 1992, and quickly grew into the largest sports radio network in the world. Wow! And all that in only twenty years!

Scorecard: 1990s

U.S. Population	248 million
President	George H. W. Bush William (Bill) J. Clinton
Major Events	Nelson Mandela Released from Prison (1990) Cold War Ends as USSR Collapses (1991) First Gulf War (1991) European Union (1992); Euro (1999) Hurricane Andrew (1992) Rodney King Beating / LA Riots (1992) NAFTA (1993) O. J. Simpson Trial (1994) Genocide in Rwanda (1994) USA Atlantis Docks with Russia Mir (1995) Dolly the Sheep Cloned (1996) Bill Clinton Impeached (1998) Columbine High School Shooting (1999)
Most Popular Sport	Football
Sports Events	Magic Johnson Retires – HIV virus (1991) USA Olympic Basketball Dream Team (1992) NHL Lockout – short season (1994-1995) Baseball Strike – 1994 World Series canceled Cal Ripken breaks Gehrig Consecutive Game record (1995) McGwire breaks Maris single season HR record (1998) U.S. Women's Soccer team wins World Cup (1999)

Sports Additions	Disney acquires ABC and ESPN (1996) ESPN's 1st Major League Baseball game (1990) WNBA Founded (1997)
New Technology	Hubble Space Telescope launched (1990) World Wide Web (WWW) debuts on the Internet (1991) WiFi (1991) Apple laptop (1991) Webcam invented (1991) 1st Smartphone (1992) 1st Text Message to mobile phone (1992) 1st Personal Digital Assistant (PDA) (1992) Mosaic browser (1992) Video Streaming (1992) U.S. Internet Banking begins (1994) Audio Streaming (1995) [ESPN baseball game] Amazon, Yahoo! (1994), eBay (1995) Digital Video Disc (DVD) (1995) Netflix (rent DVDs by mail) (1997) 1st Large Flat Screen TV (1997) AOL Instant Messenger (1997) High-Definition Television (HDTV) (1998) Google (1998) Napster (file-sharing) (1999) SD Memory card, USB Flash drive (1999)
Communications	Television Radio Newspapers Internet, World Wide Web
Average Baseball Ticket Price	$16.00

The Champions

MLB World Series

1990	Cincinnati Reds	(4-0)	v. Oakland Athletics
1991	Minnesota Twins	(4-3)	v. Atlanta Braves
1992	Toronto Blue Jays	(4-2)	v. Atlanta Braves
1993	Toronto Blue Jays	(4-2)	v. Philadelphia Phillies
1994	*No World Series – Players Strike*		
1995	Atlanta Braves	(4-2)	v. Cleveland Indians
1996	New York Yankees	(4-2)	v. Atlanta Braves
1997	Florida Marlins	(4-3)	v. Cleveland Indians
1998	New York Yankees	(4-0)	v. San Diego Padres
1999	New York Yankees	(4-0)	v. Atlanta Braves

NFL Super Bowl

1990	San Francisco 49ers	(55-10)	v. Denver Broncos
1991	New York Giants	(20-19)	v. Buffalo Bills
1992	Washington Redskins	(37-24)	v. Buffalo Bills
1993	Dallas Cowboys	(52-17)	v. Buffalo Bills
1994	Dallas Cowboys	(30-13)	v. Buffalo Bills
1995	San Francisco 49ers	(49-26)	v . San Diego Chargers
1996	Dallas Cowboys	(27-17)	v. Pittsburgh Steelers
1997	Green Bay Packers	(35-21)	v. New England Patriots
1998	Denver Broncos	(31-24)	v. Green Bay Packers
1999	Denver Broncos	(34-19)	v. Atlanta Falcons

NHL Stanley Cup

1990	Edmonton Oilers	(4-1)	v. Boston Bruins
1991	Pittsburgh Penguins	(4-2)	v. Minnesota North Stars
1992	Pittsburgh Penguins	(4-0)	v. Chicago Blackhawks
1993	Montreal Canadiens	(4-1)	v. Los Angeles Kings
1994	New York Rangers	(4-3)	v. Vancouver Canucks
1995 *	New Jersey Devils	(4-0)	v. Detroit Red Wings
1996	Colorado Avalanche	(4-0)	v. Florida Panthers

The Champions

1997	Detroit Red Wings	(4-0)	v. Philadelphia Flyers
1998	Detroit Red Wings	(4-0)	v. Washington Capitals
1999	Dallas Stars	(4-2)	v. Buffalo Sabres

** Lockout cancellation of 468 games*

NBA Championship

1990	Detroit Pistons	(4-1)	v. Portland Trail Blazers
1991	Chicago Bulls	(4-1)	v. Los Angeles Lakers
1992	Chicago Bulls	(4-2)	v. Portland Trail Blazers
1993	Chicago Bulls	(4-2)	v. Phoenix Suns
1994	Houston Rockets	(4-3)	v. New York Knicks
1995	Houston Rockets	(4-0)	v. Orlando Magic
1996	Chicago Bulls	(4-2)	v. Seattle SuperSonics
1997	Chicago Bulls	(4-2)	v. Utah Jazz
1998	Chicago Bulls	(4-2)	v. Utah Jazz
1999	San Antonio Spurs	(4-1)	v. New York Knicks

WNBA Championship

1990			
1991			
1992			
1993			
1994			
1995			
1996			
1997	Houston Comets	(1-0)	v. New York Liberty
1998	Houston Comets	(2-1)	v. Phoenix Mercury
1999	Houston Comets	(2-1)	v. New York Liberty

The Champions

NCAA College Football

1990	Colorado / Georgia Tech
1991	Washington / Miami (Fla)
1992	Alabama
1993	Florida State
1994	Nebraska
1995	Nebraska
1996	Florida
1997	Michigan / Nebraska
1998	Tennessee
1999	Florida State

Heisman Trophy

1990	Ty Detmer	QB	BYU
1991	Desmond Howard	WR/PR	Michigan
1992	Gino Torrettas	QB	Miami
1993	Charlie Ward	QB	Florida State
1994	Rashaan Salaam	RB	Colorado
1995	Eddie George	RB	Ohio State
1996	Danny Wuerffel	QB	Florida
1997	Charles Woodson	CB	Michigan
1998	Ricky Williams	HB	Texas
1999	Ron Dayne	RB	Wisconsin

The Champions

NCAA College World Series

		Baseball Men		Softball Women
1990		Georgia (52-19)		UCLA (62-7)
1991	*	LSU (55-18)		Arizona (56-16)
1992	*	Pepperdine (48-11-1)	*	UCLA (54-2)
1993		LSU (53-17-1)		Arizona (44-8)
1994	*	Oklahoma (50-17)	*	Arizona (64-3)
1995	*	Cal St. Fullerton (57-9)	*#	UCLA (50-6)
1996	*	LSU (52-15)	*	Arizona (58-9)
1997	*	LSU (57-13)		Arizona (61-5)
1998		Southern California (49-17)		Fresno State (52-11)
1999	*	Miami (Fla.) (50-13)	*	UCLA (63-6)

** Indicates undefeated teams in College World Series play.*
 # Title later vacated by Committee on infractions.

NCAA College Basketball

	Men	Women
1990	UNLV (35-5)	Stanford (32-1)
1991	Duke (32-7)	Tennessee (30-5)
1992	Duke (34-2)	Stanford (30-3)
1993	North Carolina (34-4)	Texas Tech (31-3)
1994	Arkansas (34-3)	North Carolina (33-2)
1995	UCLA (31-2)	Connecticut (35-0)
1996	Kentucky (34-2)	Tennessee (32-4)
1997	Arizona (25-9)	Tennessee (29-10)
1998	Kentucky (35-4)	Tennessee (39-0)
1999	Connecticut (34-2)	Purdue (34-1)

Tiger Woods

The 2000s

I was in Hilton Head, South Carolina, on the morning of September 11, 2001. My son, Scott, called and asked if I knew what had just happened. I turned on the television just in time to see United Flight 175 crash into the South Tower of the World Trade Center. "What was that?" I asked Scott. "I think it was another airplane," he replied. "About 15 minutes ago, a plane (American Flight 11) crashed into the other tower." An hour and a half later, American Flight 77 flew into the Pentagon and, thirty minutes after that United Flight 93, which was headed for Washington DC, crashed in the countryside of Western Pennsylvania. Passengers and crew on that plane were on the phones and had heard about the other attacks. So they heroically fought to overtake the four hijackers. And the Twin Towers both collapsed, making Lower Manhattan look like a war zone.

Watching all this took me back to Pearl Harbor on December 7, 1941 – another sneak attack in broad daylight. Sixty years earlier, I was nine years old and in the fourth grade. But 9/11 gave me the same sickening feeling – and I couldn't help but recall when my father sat us all down in front of the radio to hear President Roosevelt's "day of infamy" speech to Congress.

These horrendous terrorist attacks on American soil were tough starts to the new decade – actually, the new millennium. But I was proud to see how sports helped shape our national response. Major League Baseball, the National Football League, and college football were all put on hold, as were most sporting events. Athletes spoke of their unwillingness to move too quickly, citing a responsibility to honor and help the victims and their families. And many professional athletes donated a significant part of their salaries for relief aid. All our sports, of course, did come back in the days and weeks after 9/11. And when they did, they helped the nation heal, uplifted our spirits, and gave us something to be happy about again.

Mike Piazza hit a dramatic game winning home run in the first baseball game played in New York after the 9/11 attacks

On September 21, 2001, in the first sporting event in New York City since the attacks, the New York Mets hosted the Atlanta Braves at Shea Stadium. In the bottom of the 8th inning, with the home team trailing 2-1, Mike Piazza hit a memorable home run to give the Mets a 3-2 comeback win. The stadium crowd exploded in an emotional display the likes of which had rarely been experienced at a regular-season sporting event. A month later, the New York Yankees made it to the World Series, where President Bush threw out the first pitch in a symbolic display of patriotism. And the Yankees won each game played in New York.

You may have heard of Rasmussen Reports, the polling company that collects and publishes public information on politics, current events, consumer-related, business topics, and presidential job-approval ratings. Well, that's my son, Scott. He got started by making phone calls to do polling for several corporate clients in the Chicago area. Back then, he called his company Portrait of America. For a major bank, he performed internal polling of employees (likes, dislikes, job satisfaction, etc.). That quickly expanded to external polling that tracked employment status, mortgage information, and other topics vital to the banking industry. Soon he expanded to political polling for local congressional races across several states – both on issues, such as term limits, and a candidate's standing in the races. In 2003, business was going so well that Scott decided to incorporate and rename the company Rasmussen Reports.

I moved back to New Jersey to help Scott with the increased demand, which came from the presidential election year. A family friend would also join the company to handle the extra workload and my daughter, Lynn, was brought on as a backup. I would get up at 5 a.m. every morning to process the overnight data, put the numbers into his proprietary computer program, and then I'd go for a walk on the beach at 6 o'clock. Scott would analyze the data and have all the new information published by 9 a.m. With the many state and national races that year, Rasmussen Reports really picked up steam. And when Scott's numbers for the Bush-Kerry race came out right on the money, demand took off like a rocket. Recognizing the accuracy and quality of his work, Scott was named by the *Wall Street Journal* as one of the most accurate and influential political pollsters in America. Later, they described him as "America's Insurgent Pollster" and a "key player in the contact sport of politics." The *Washington Post* called Scott "a driving force in American politics." He has written and published six books.

Also, in 2004, on September 7, I was invited to a celebration of ESPN's 25th anniversary. George Bodenheimer, then president, went out of his way to ask my wife and me to attend, which pleasantly surprised me because I had been away from ESPN for so long. The gala was held in New York City at the ESPN Zone – a massive theme restaurant in Times Square. All the

ESPN's 25th anniversary was held at the ESPN Zone (L) in New York City. George Bodenheimer (R), who worked his way from the mail room to the senior executive, invited me back into the ESPN family after a long absence

former presidents and executives attended, including Stu Evey and Chet Simmons. Disney executives like Bob Iger also showed up. George and some of the other notables got up and said a few words marking the occasion. The Dallas Cowboy Cheerleaders performed, and the company handed out a special commemorative book. Basically it was one big party, which I thoroughly enjoyed – especially since I seemed to have been persona non grata for so long. But George Bodenheimer changed all that. He was then, and is now, a class guy.

Following the success of Rasmussen Reports, I grew restless and it was time to scratch that entrepreneurial itch again. Websites had begun adding social networking elements that allowed users to post comments and enhance the user experience with personalized content. I recognized how this new technology presented an opportunity to deliver yet another layer of sports information and entertainment to millions of passionate fans.

While brainstorming with Lynn Daniels, the family friend who worked with us during the presidential election, we came up with a concept that integrated sports with the new social networking components. She handled operations, finance and technology and I stuck to the overall business management and sports. Lynn and I raised $5.3 million from several investors and, in early 2007, we created a company called College Fanz Sports Network. Our new network included every college and university team in the National Collegiate Athletic Association (NCAA), the National Association of Intercollegiate Athletics (NAIA), National Christian College Athletic Association (NCCAA), and United States College Athletic Association (USCAA) – over 1,450 of them, including a few in Canada. We launched College Fanz in June, 2008 at the annual convention of College Sports Information Directors of America (CoSIDA). I was 75 years old and felt like a kid again.

We were introduced to OpenCrowd, the best technology company in New York. They came highly recommended, having developed the website MLB.com and a key website in the financial sector. They incorporated all the elements we needed and Lynn enhanced the database so that every team page showcased the team colors and nicknames, their mascots, schedules, and standings. We gave the fans a place to support their favorite teams and players. She even made sure the band had its rightful place among the fans. We included details on every team. Did you know, for example, that the nickname for the men at the University of Arkansas at Monticello is the Boll Weevils, but the women are the Cotton Blossoms? We also kept track of more than 225,000 web pages – and added a live feed of the team schedules and results. Then we expanded the fans' experience with a patented "Virtual Pressbox®" that allowed each school's Sports Information Director to update scores in real-time and even add weather conditions and delays. In addition, fans posted their videos and photos on their team page, voted for their favorite teams and players, participated in trivia quizzes, and communicated with other fans. Essentially, it was the first college sports social network and, for a time, the largest in the world. People participated from over 100 countries and from every corner of the United States.

College Fanz Sports Network went border-to-border and coast-to-coast

In 2009, we acquired a small business focused exclusively on NAIA sports, purchased television production equipment, travel vans, brought in announcers and color commentators, and hit the road to broadcast football and basketball games that other networks did not cover. We were the first to produce this magnitude of small college sporting events live streamed over the Internet. When we showed up at a school, we made it a big event, borrowing from ESPN's Game Day. We arrived a day early to recruit 8 or 9 students, both male and female, and teach them how to run the cameras. They helped put banners around the field and create an exciting and thrilling experience for the fans. Enthusiasm at the small colleges was absolutely fantastic. College Fanz sponsored the NAIA football and basketball Game of the Week, published an NAIA Football Preview magazine and ranked the teams.

And then I learned that the NAIA had the oldest basketball tournament in the nation (1937) *and* that it wasn't being televised! So we cut a deal to live stream games from both the men's and women's tournaments, which showcased 128 teams at the end of the 2009 season. Together, the men's and women's basketball tournaments were played at the same time in two different cities over five days. That is a staggering logistical feat. [Having done basketball scheduling for the Big Ten in the 1980s, I knew how complicated it was. Simply amazing!]

That led us to covering the NAIA football championship series, which reminded me of the first games ESPN covered in 1979. Back then, we did not have live television rights to NCAA football games, but our reporters had access to the sidelines during the game being televised by ABC, NBC, or CBS. So we recorded sideline footage, held interviews and did everything except televise the game. Our reporters were in bright red jackets with the logo on the back in huge white letters and instructed to position themselves on the home sideline, facing the field. That way, despite their attitude toward ESPN, the major networks ended up promoting us! Almost every play in their broadcast included the ESPN logo. CBS, in particular, wasn't happy with us. Later that day, adding insult to injury, we included the game highlights in the evening SportsCenter shows.

In addition to showcasing small college sports, we found another way to give back - we formed the College Fanz Scholarship Fund. All proceeds from the merchandise sales at the games were donated to the teams. This was an important way for me to pay it forward and fulfill a passion of mine. Not only did I attend DePauw on a scholarship, I also earned my MBA from Rutgers on a scholarship. If they were not available to me, my path would have been *completely* different. My desire has

The College Fanz Scholarship Fund fulfilled one of my dreams

always been to provide a similar opportunity for others.

Our March Madness contests were another first. We offered $1 million for a perfect bracket as well as prizes for the closest brackets in all 6 NCAA men's and women's championships and all 4 NAIA men's and women's championships [for a total of 10 winners]. Nobody had a perfect bracket, but we sent the top contest winner on an all-expense-paid trip to Hawaii for the Maui Classic. That was a lot of fun.

There were so many firsts with this project and momentum built with each game as fans found a place to support their teams. Colleges were already planning for the next season. The enthusiasm was infectious and College Fanz was on track to be a great success.

Suddenly, our lead investor lost interest. I offered to sell the company to ESPN, but was unsuccessful. By the middle of 2010, Lynn and I brought the company to a cash-positive conclusion as he shut down the business and fired everybody [including his son-in-law, that he had installed as president two years earlier].

At the end of the decade, sports were as strong as ever. New York debuted a new Yankee Stadium where the Yanks won their 27th World Series. But I think one of the biggest events of the 2000s was when the Boston Red Sox swept the St. Louis Cardinals, 4-0, to win the World Series in 2004 – and before that, winning four games in a row in the ALCS to overcome a 3-0 deficit to beat the Yankees. That was the only time in baseball that any team had ever come back from that kind of post-season deficit. The Red Sox hadn't won it all in 86 years – not since they sold Babe Ruth to the Yankees for $125,000. That ended the so-called superstitious Curse of the Bambino, which believers said was inflicted on Boston for letting Ruth go.

David Ortiz led the 2004 Red Sox to a World Series win, breaking the 86 year drought known as the "Curse of the Bambino"

Scorecard: 2000s

U.S. Population	281 million
President	William (Bill) J. Clinton George W. Bush Barack Obama
Major Events	Presidential Election Controversy: Hanging Chads (2000) 9/11 Attacks on World Trade Center, Pentagon (9/11/2001) War in Afghanistan begins (2001) Dot com Bubble Burst (2001) Iraq War (2003-2011) Hurricane Katrina (2005) Bitcoin (2008) The Great Recession (2007-2009) Tea Party Movement (2009)
Most Popular Sport	Football
Sports Events	Barry Bonds breaks single season Home Run record (2001) Red Sox win World Series; break Curse of the Bambino (2004) NHL Season Lockout (2005) Congress Investigates Drug use in Sports (2005) Bonds breaks Aaron's career Home Run record (2007) Tiger Woods holds all Golf major titles at once (2008-2009) Usain Bolt breaks Olympic 100-meter & 200-meter records (2008)

New Technology	World's 1st Telesurgery (2001) Apple iPod (2001) Skype video conferencing (2003) Android (mobile phone operating system) (2003) Full DNA Human Genome Sequence revealed (2003) Spirit Rover lands on Mars (2004) Web 2.0 (social networking) (2004) Facebook (2004) YouTube (online video streaming) (2005) 3D Light Detection and Ranging (LiDAR) Scanner (2005) LCD flat screen TV (2006) MySpace 1st instant messaging platform in a social network (2006) Twitter (2006) Cloud data storage (2006) Apple iPhone (2007) Flat Panel Computer displays (2007)
Communications	Television Radio Internet / World Wide Web Newspapers
Average Baseball Ticket Price	$32.00

The Champions

MLB World Series

2000	New York Yankees	(4-1)	v. New York Mets
2001	Arizona Diamondbacks	(4-1)	v. New York Yankees
2002	Anaheim Angels	(4-3)	v. San Francisco Giants
2003	Florida Marlins	(4-2)	v. New York Yankees
2004	Boston Red Sox	(4-0)	v. St. Louis Cardinals
2005	Chicago White Sox	(4-0)	v. Houston Astros
2006	St. Louis Cardinals	(4-1)	v. Detroit Tigers
2007	Boston Red Sox	(4-0)	v. Colorado Rockies
2008	Philadelphia Phillies	(4-1)	v. Tampa Bay Rays
2009	New York Yankees	(4-2)	v. Philadelphia Phillies

NFL Super Bowl

2000	St. Louis Rams	(23-16)	v. Tennessee Titans
2001	Baltimore Ravens	(34-7)	v. New York Giants
2002	New England Patriots	(20-17)	v. St. Louis Rams
2003	Tampa Bay Buccaneers	(48-21)	v. Oakland Raiders
2004	New England Patriots	(32-29)	v. Carolina Panthers
2005	New England Patriots	24-21)	v. Philadelphia Eagles
2006	Pittsburgh Steelers	(21-10)	v. Seattle Seahawks
2007	Indianapolis Colts	(29-17)	v. Chicago Bears
2008	New York Giants	(17-14)	v. New England Patriots
2009	Pittsburgh Steelers	(27-23)	v. Arizona Cardinals

NHL Stanley Cup

2000	New Jersey Devils	(4-2)	v. Dallas Stars
2001	Colorado Avalanche	(4-3)	v. New Jersey Devils
2002	Detroit Red Wings	(4-1)	v. Carolina Hurricanes
2003	New Jersey Devils	(4-3)	v. Mighty Ducks / Anaheim
2004	Tampa Bay Lightning	(4-3)	v. Calgary Flames
2005	*Season cancelled due to the 2004-05 NHL lockout*		
2006	Carolina Hurricanes	(4-3)	v. Edmonton Oilers

The Champions

2007	Anaheim Ducks	(4-1)	v. Ottawa Senators
2008	Detroit Red Wings	(4-2)	v. Pittsburgh Penguins
2009	Pittsburgh Penguins	(4-3)	v. Detroit Red Wings

NBA Championship

2000	Los Angeles Lakers	(4-2)	v. Indiana Pacers
2001	Los Angeles Lakers	(4-1)	v. Philadelphia 76ers
2002	Los Angeles Lakers	(4-0)	v. New Jersey Nets
2003	San Antonio Spurs	(4-2)	v. New Jersey Nets
2004	Detroit Pistons	(4-1)	v. Los Angeles Lakers
2005	San Antonio Spurs	(4-3)	v. Detroit Pistons
2006	Miami Heat	(4-2)	v. Dallas Mavericks
2007	San Antonio Spurs	(4-0)	v. Cleveland Cavaliers
2008	Boston Celtics	(4-2)	v. Los Angeles Lakers
2009	Los Angeles Lakers	(4-1)	v. Orlando Magic

WNBA Championship

2000	Houston Comets	(2-0)	v. New York Liberty
2001	Los Angeles Sparks	(2-0)	v. Charlotte Sting
2002	Los Angeles Sparks	(2-0)	v. New York Liberty
2003	Detroit Shock	(2-1)	v. Los Angeles Sparks
2004	Seattle Storm	(2-1)	v. Connecticut Sun
2005	Sacramento Monarchs	(3-1)	v. Connecticut Sun
2006	Detroit Shock	(3-2)	v. Sacramento Monarchs
2007	Phoenix Mercury	(3-2)	v. Detroit Shock
2008	Detroit Shock	(3-0)	v. San Antonio Silver Stars
2009	Phoenix Mercury	(3-2)	v. Indiana Fever

The Champions

NCAA College Football

2000	Oklahoma
2001	Miami (Fla)
2002	Ohio State
2003	LSU / USC
2004 *	USC
2005	Texas
2006	Florida
2007	LSU
2008	Florida
2009	Alabama

** Southern California's participation in the 2004 championship was vacated by the NCAA Committee on Infractions.*

Heisman Trophy

2000	Chris Weinke	QB	Florida State
2001	Eric Crouch	QB	Nebraska
2002	Carson Palmer	QB	USC
2003	Jason White	QB	Oklahoma
2004	Matt Leinart	QB	USC
2005	*Reggie Bush (Vacated)*	RB	USC
2006	Troy Smith	QB	Ohio State
2007	Tim Tebow	QB	Florida
2008	Sam Bradford	QB	Oklahoma
2009	Mark Ingram, Jr.	RB	Alabama

The Champions

NCAA College World Series

Year		Baseball *Men*		Softball *Women*
2000	*	LSU (52-17)	*	Oklahoma (66-8)
2001	*	Miami (Fla.) (53-12)	*	Arizona (65-4)
2002	*	Texas (57-15)		California (56-19)
2003		Rice (58-12)		UCLA (54-7)
2004		Cal St. Fullerton (47-22)		UCLA (47-9)
2005	*	Texas (56-16)		Michigan (65-7)
2006		Oregon State (50-16)		Arizona (54-11)
2007	*	Oregon State 49-18)		Arizona (50-14-1)
2008		Fresno State (47-31)	*	Arizona State (66-5)
2009		LSU (56-17)		Washington (51-12)

**Indicates undefeated teams in College World Series play.*

NCAA College Basketball

Year	*Men*	*Women*
2000	Michigan State (32-7)	Connecticut (36-1)
2001	Duke (35-4)	Notre Dame (34-2)
2002	Maryland (32-4)	Connecticut (39-0)
2003	Syracuse (30-5)	Connecticut (37-1)
2004	Connecticut (33-6)	Connecticut (31-4)
2005	North Carolina (33-4)	Baylor (33-3)
2006	Florida (33-6)	Maryland (34-4)
2007	Florida (35-5)	Tennessee (34-3)
2008	Kansas (37-3)	Tennessee (36-2)
2009	North Carolina (34-3)	Connecticut (39-0)

Tom Brady

The 2010s

September 7, 2010 was ESPN's 31st anniversary. George Bodenheimer had invited me to Bristol to join in the celebration. On that day, a small ceremony was held to dedicate a new flagpole to me "*in honor of his entrepreneurial spirit and passion for sports.*"

Flagpole Dedicated to Bill Rasmussen on ESPN's 31st Anniversary

Several years later, the flagpole was taken down, but the plaque is still there. It was a really wonderful gesture and I very much appreciated it, especially since I was slowing down as the new decade started.

People were still approaching me to start up new business ventures. I was asked, for instance, to do a radio sports show, because, as they said: "Your history goes back so far and you remember everything." I thought about it, but it just wasn't meant to be at that late stage of my life.

I was also being asked to speak quite a bit – and I did a couple of commencement addresses. One day I received a call from a speaker's bureau telling me that Chris Berman couldn't make an event and he recommended I go in his place. It was the annual meeting of a company that operates barges on the Ohio and Mississippi Rivers. So I went to Louisville, had a great time, was well-received – and I got paid a few thousand dollars. So I decided to add more speaking engagements and I was pleased to discover how many colleges and organizations wanted to hear me speak.

Today, speaking opportunities take me to business conferences, conventions, and symposiums. On the collegiate circuit, honors classes, sports management classes, and business schools take a special interest, including schools such as Wharton at the University of Pennsylvania and Kellogg at Northwestern University. After I tell the ESPN story, we always have a question and answer session. These audiences are particularly curious about my background and education, and I am pleased to be able to tell them I have a degree in economics from DePauw and an MBA from Rutgers. And almost always, I'm asked, "How did you finance this thing? How did you make ESPN happen?"

My response is, "Well, it was easy. A $9,000 credit card cash advance and $145 million from Getty. Voila! Instant Network." That always gets a laugh.

In addition to business conferences and corporate events, a number of my speaking engagements have been at major universities – Auburn, Oklahoma, Minnesota, Florida, Villanova, Kansas, and UConn, to name just a few. My alma mater, DePauw, asked me back several times and on one of those trips I was Executive in Residence at the Robert C. McDermond Center for Management and Entrepreneurship.

The college audiences are really fun and they ask me a lot of questions. What sport did I play? (*Baseball*) What is my favorite sport? (*Baseball*) So you really know Chris Berman? (*Yes*) Once I was asked how we picked all the announcers when we got started. And I told them that when we first announced that we were forming an all-sports network (in 1978), we quickly received 2,500 videocassette tapes – each one with a profile of a potential sports announcer. We invited those who followed up with a phone call to come in for a tryout. Some showed up, but most didn't.

Wherever I go, the most frequent question I receive (by far) is, "Why Bristol?"

"We began in Plainville, Connecticut," I'd say, "and we were going to put up several large satellite dishes. But the Plainville Town Council passed an ordinance prohibiting satellite dishes inside town limits. So we moved across the street to Bristol and

Plainville, Connecticut, prohibited satellite dishes, so we moved across the street to Bristol

purchased one acre of a five-acre redevelopment site." [It used to be a dump.] When we first visited that site, we were standing in mud and grass when somebody looked at the paperwork and noticed that the mailing address was 935 Middle Street. "Well, that's just another everyday address," I said. So we went down to the post office and asked if we could rename it ESPN Plaza (zip code 06010).

And they said, "Sure!" Eventually, that one acre turned into 123 acres and our initial 5,000 square foot building turned into 19 buildings with 1.3 million square feet. I believe it's safe to say that our company really transformed Bristol, Connecticut. ESPN has been a good corporate citizen to the community by building parks, daycare centers, and all kinds of other good things. And now, ESPN pays more taxes than the next 10 businesses combined. Poor Plainville.

Bristol: sports capital of the world!

When I'm at colleges and universities, I always volunteer to speak to smaller groups of students. For example, in 2009, on the College Fanz tour, I spoke to groups on each campus we visited on Game Day. And then I remember one time at an honors class at the University of Texas when I noticed a young man who seemed like he wanted to talk, but was a little too shy. So I asked him where he was from. "Venezuela," he said.

The ESPN Mission Statement displayed for all the world to see. Business classes are surprised at the impact of these 6 simple words

And I replied, "Oh, Luis Aparicio and Chico Carrasquel!"

His face just lit up. "Do you know them?" he asked.

"Not personally, but they both played in Chicago – and I'm from Chicago."

This young man followed me out to my car when the class was over, shook my hand, and said, "You won't remember my name. But you watch, you watch. You'll recognize my face. You've been so inspiring to me. One day I will be a CEO."

I've always thought that sports was the great conversation icebreaker. And it certainly was the case for this shy young man. After I met him, I started ending my talks by saying: "If just one person walks out of here motivated by anything I've said – today has been a success."

In 2011, my wife, Lois Ann McDonell (Mickey) passed away at the age of 77. It was three days before our 56th wedding anniversary (we were married in 1955). In the hospital to have some tests run, she had lost some weight, become a bit frail, and was suffering from emphysema. I had gone to see her that morning and she reminded me of a meeting I had out of town, which was on the day of our anniversary. "Well, I'm not going," I said.

"Oh, no. You go," she insisted.

"I'm not going to go," I said. Then she asked me to deposit a check for her, and I told her I'd do that right away and would call her in a little while. So I went to the bank and then phoned to tell her that I was back home.

My wife, Mickey, was a Yankee fan through and through her entire life

"Oh, by the way, how did the Yankees do?" she asked. [Mickey was a New York Yankees fan, through and through. Her father (born and raised in Boston) loved the Red Sox, and from the first grade, she squabbled with him about which team was better.]

"They beat the Reds," I replied.

"Who got the win?"

"Freddie Garcia."

"Good for Freddie," she said.

And those were the last words she ever spoke. She just stopped talking.

I thought that was odd, so I immediately called the hospital. "The nurses are already in there," I was told. "Come quickly."

She had just been served lunch – and they found her with the phone in her left hand and a fork in her right hand. She actually died while I was speaking with her on the phone. I was stunned. I just couldn't believe it. But I can look back on it now and appreciate that she was a sports fan (and a fierce Yankee fan) right to the very end. Our sons, Scott, Glenn, and grandson, Andy, put together a video for her memorial service that featured the song "You Gotta Have Heart" from the play *Damn Yankees*. It was appropriate and very touching.

In 2014, I was experiencing a little twitch in my left hand and arm. So I went in to see a neurologist at the University of Washington Medical Center who put me through a series of special exercises and then ordered an MRI. At the next appointment, my daughter, Lynn, who is an oncology nurse, was with me when Dr. James Gordon came in and told us he had bad news. "You have Parkinson's," he said.

And my daughter immediately breathed a sigh of relief and said, "Oh, good!" [She thought I might have had brain cancer.]

But the doctor was also very encouraging. "Look, you'll die *with* Parkinson's, not *from* it," he said. "We've got medication that will help slow the progression of the disease. Our aim is to control and manage it so you can carry on a normal life. If you exercise your body and brain and stay active, you should be just fine. Some people live with it for years and years and years."

In 2016, a local television sports announcer asked me to do an interview. Muhammad Ali (who also had Parkinson's) had just passed away and he wanted to hear my memories of "The Greatest." I recounted the 1965 press conference just before the second Sonny Liston fight – and how Ali had come down beforehand and just sat down and chatted with me for 30 to 45 minutes. I said a lot of nice things about him. And made sure to remark that as big as he was to the sports world, he was just as good and decent a human being.

In 2016, the Chicago Cubs won their first World Series in 108 years, and my hometown celebrated like never before

This decade was memorable in sports. In 2016, the Chicago Cubs won their first World Series in 108 years – and the Boston Bruins won their first Stanley Cup in 40 years (2011). Television and the Internet/ Social Media had surpassed radio in mass communications. And paper newspapers were almost gone.

Football was still the most popular sport in the United States and, I'm proud to say that ESPN secured the rights to televise the College Football Playoff, which began in 2015. By 2019, more than 350 cameras were used for the megacast on multiple ESPN platforms, including radio, video, cable, live streaming, and ABC. It really was a new era in sports and technology. By the end of the decade, nearly all the sports conferences had their own networks, including the SEC, Big Ten, PAC 12, Big 12, and the ACC (three of which are in partnership with ESPN). And many individual schools, such as the University of Texas, had also created their own sports networks. They all do streaming now.

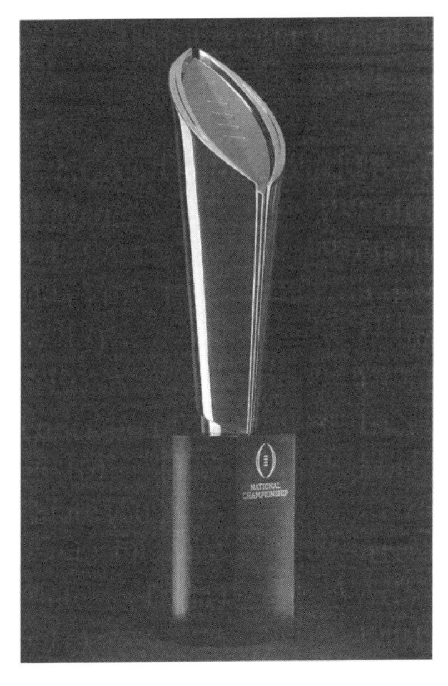

College Football Playoff National Championship Trophy

2019 marked ESPN's 40th anniversary. To celebrate, the network executives asked me to go on a tour, speak to employees, and do some press. So I traveled to Charlotte, New York City, Boston's Fenway Park (where I threw out the first pitch on ESPN Sunday Night Baseball), Los Angeles, and, of course, Bristol. On September 7th, ESPN held a town hall on campus. More than 1,000 people attended – a crowd so large that an air-conditioned tent structure had to be erected. Jimmy Pitaro, ESPN's president, opened the meeting. He mentioned that he was ten years old when ESPN debuted and that he sat in his basement watching SportsCenter so often that his parents got after him to stop. I was sitting in the front row, and when Jimmy introduced me and asked me to stand, I was amazed that I was honored with a standing ovation. It was sustained, too, with lots of cheering. Talk about an emotional moment for me. Wow!

Later in the program, six current and former SportsCenter hosts were about to speak about their time at ESPN. Bob Ley, Chris Berman, Mike Tirico, Suzy Kolber, Robin Roberts, and Dan Patrick started for the stage when Berman told the others that first, he was going over to me. [Berman always called me "George," because he said I was the George Washington of ESPN.] So he took a right turn and everybody followed him. They all shook my hand and gave me a hug. And when the audience saw that display of respect and gratitude, they rose to their feet again – another standing ovation.

It was a very, very moving moment – one that will stay with me for the rest of my life.

Photo Album

Walk with me through the highlights of my time at ESPN. Starting in 1978 when I was fired by the New England Whalers, putting it all together in 14 short months until Opening Night, where we all held our breaths, knowing it was being directed and produced from the remote truck parked outside. Fast forward to ESPN's spectacular 40th anniversary that was celebrated in style over a long period of time, in several different locations with lots of employees. I threw out the first pitch when the Yankees played the Red Sox in Fenway Park and Jimmy Pitaro was my catcher. There were still a number of employees who started working with me the very first year! A lot of my favorite people helped me celebrate at different locations around the country.

After those pages, I'll take you through some of my favorite memories before and after ESPN.

Opening Night Jitters - *Remembering that very first night we went on the air on September 7th, 1979 at 7:00 pm Eastern, nobody knew what would happen. Nobody knew we had to cut a hole in the back wall to run cables out to the muddy field where the remote truck handled the actual transmission to the satellite*

ESPN's first 6 Presidents Bill Rasmussen, Chet Simmons, Bill Grimes, Roger Werner, Steve Bornstein and George Bodenheimer at the 25th anniversary in New York City. This was a huge milestone for me

ESPN celebrated the 30th anniversary at home in Bristol where I spent time with Young Reporters and the 35th was celebrated at the Paley Center for Media in New York City where George Grande and Robin Rogerts celebrated with me. The flag pole was dedicated to me on the 31st anniversary and George Bodenheimer, Bob Ley, and Chris Berman shared the day with me

These are 33 of the original 80 employees still working at ESPN on the 31st anniversary. Many could not imagine working anywhere else!

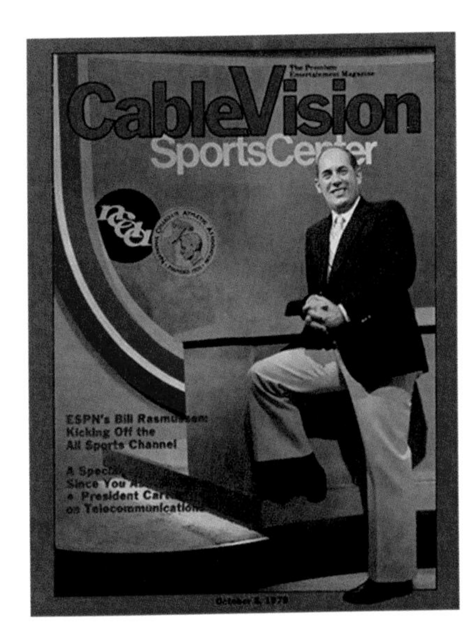

CableVision magazine wrote about 'ESPN's Bill Rasmussen Kicking Off the All Sports Channel' in October 1979, displaying the original SportsCenter set, featuring the NCAA logo. ESPN's work was recognized by the major networks on the 35th anniversary and I was asked to pose on the first SportsCenter set. I didn't recognize it because their rendition was not correct! Here I am with Mike Tirico and Jimmy Pitaro on the remake for the 40th anniversary, which was 7 years after the 50,000th SportsCenter show aired

On ESPN's 40th anniversary, in a sign of love and respect, Chris Berman led five SportsCenter hosts over to me at the Town Hall event. Robin Roberts and Mike Tirico shared treasured moments with me. George Bodenheimer and George Grande had front row seats. The Fab 5: Bill with Chris LaPlaca, Bob Ley, George Bodenheimer and Mike Soltys

I celebrated ESPN's 40th anniversary when I threw out the first pitch at Fenway Park before the Red Sox hosted the Yankees. Jimmy Pitaro was my catcher portraying the ultimate "then" and "now". The communications team joined us for the occasion, where Josh Krulewitz, Chris LaPlaca, and Mike Soltys made sure we were in the right place at the right time

Many employees shared stories of our journey together over the 40 years. We had cake in Charlotte, New York, Bristol and Los Angeles and I got to cut them all! Presidents George Bodenheimer and Jimmy Pitaro shared cake with me. Other favorite memories include meeting Jimmy, throwing out the first pitch for the 30th anniversary and taking in a Yankee's game where I met the entire production crew

The most amazing people I know work at ESPN. Carrie Brzezinski and Rosa Gatti came to share the Cynopsis Lifetime Achievement award ceremony with me in 2016. Scottie Connel and Evan Baker shared a moment with me on in 1979. What would basketball on ESPN be without Dickie V? We only hired the very best, such as veteran sports icons Jim Simpson & Bud Wilkinson. There are so many more and not enough pages in this book to show you each and everyone who contributed to the success of ESPN. I can tell you it took every single person to make it work and I am so very proud of each and everyone who came along for the journey

First production truck 1979

Bill's first pitch in Philadelphia 2009 *First pitch in Seattle 2018*

I love what they've done with the NFL studio!

The spot on the UConn campus where Mike Soltys and I met 32 years earlier when he was hired as our first intern

There were lots of people we contracted with for all kinds of jobs but Mike Soltys was our very first intern, a title he is proud to hold as a senior executive today.

Contemplating all the miracles that made it all possible

From the people to the technology to the timing and location, ESPN was a series of miracles. The engineer from Scientific Atlanta said the site couldn't have been better: the height of the Litchfield mountains blocked interference from communications between New York City and New England, ***and*** *we had a 2 degree clearance between the uplink in Bristol and the satellite south of Hawaii. There were more miracles than I can possibly count*

Bill at the DePauw University boulder as a Freshman in 1950

Bill at the DePauw boulder during 2017 Week in Residence

My four years at DePauw University opened my eyes to a whole new world. Studying economics and geology gave me a great start, fed my passion for history and technology, as well as my life-long love of sports and competition. I cherish those years with all my classmates and instructors.

THE TIMOTHY AND SHARON UBBEN LECTURE SERIES

BILL RASMUSSEN '54

Founder of ESPN, the first 24-hour sports television network

"Finding Your Passion, Realizing Your Dreams"

Wednesday, Nov. 8, 2017 • 7:30 p.m.
Green Center for the Performing Arts, Kresge Auditorium

Book signing following the lecture
Green Center for the Performing Arts, Great Hall

All Ubben Lectures are presented free of admission charge

If you have questions about access, wish to request a sign language interpreter or accommodations for a disability, contact juliannsmith@depauw.edu before Monday, Oct. 30, 2017

Bill presents the Ubben Lecture in 2017

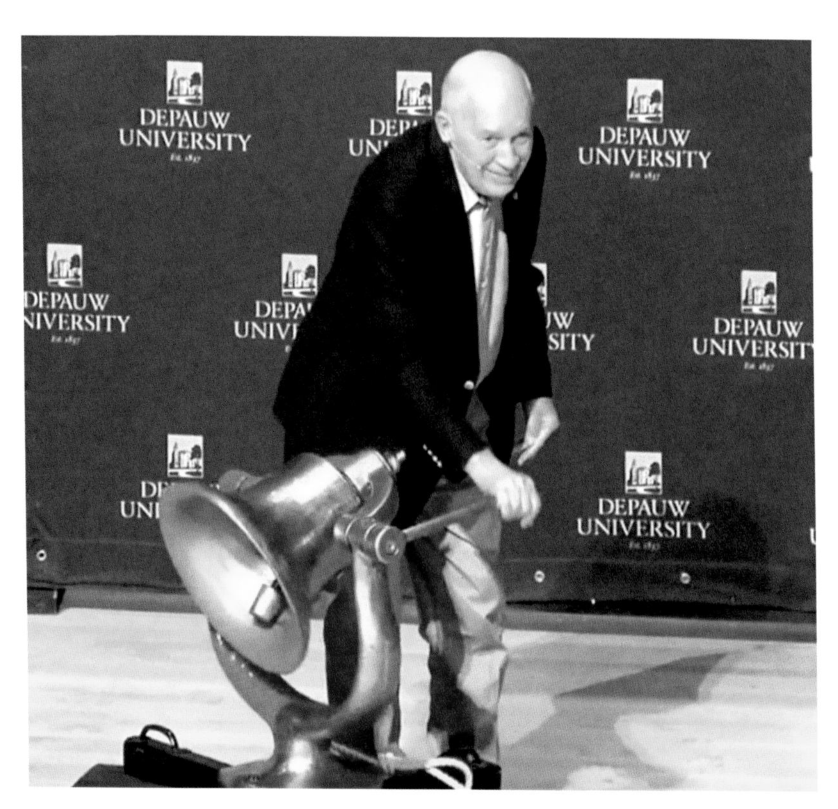

Bill rings the Monon Bell at DePauw in 2017

Delivering keynote address at the Centennial celebration of Lambda Chi Alpha, Bill's college fraternity, in 2009

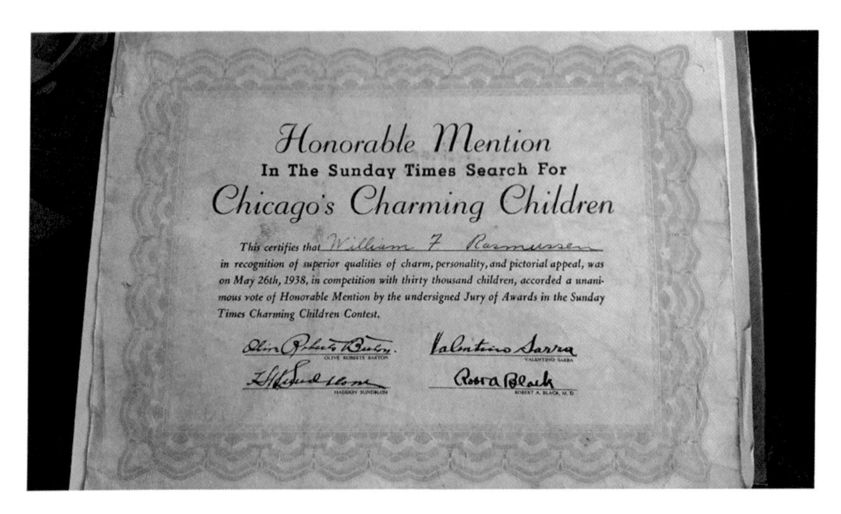

Honorable Mention

In The Sunday Times Search For

Chicago's Charming Children

This certifies that William F Rasmussen in recognition of superior qualities of charm, personality, and pictorial appeal, was on May 26th, 1938, in competition with thirty thousand children, accorded a unanimous vote of Honorable Mention by the undersigned Jury of Awards in the Sunday Times Charming Children Contest.

OLIVE ROBERTS BARTON — VALENTINO SARRA

HADDON SUNDBLOM — ROBERT A. BLACK, M.D.

Charming at age six in 1938

My mother was proud of her Charming Child at age 6 and again 10 years later when I won the Sun Times essay contest. Two years later I was granted a Rector Scholarship to DePauw, making her proud one more time.

Preparing to throw the green flag to start the NASCAR Xfinity race in Mobile, Alabama in 2016

Sharing tips with NASCAR Xfinity driver Kyle Benjamin in 2016

Bill in Groton CT 2016

With three of my granddaughters in 2016

My family has always been central to my achievements. My parents pushed me to excel in school and in sports. My children have all worked with me in one endeavor or another. My grandchildren like the attention that comes with their Pop Pop but mostly they just treat me as their own special Grandfather. Now that I have a great grandchild, life keeps getting sweeter each and every year.

My interests include officiating baseball, softball and hockey as umpire and referee over many years

A favorite memoir from 1979

Stirring displays of giant American flags at sports events throughout the country touch millions of fans every year. Fans in the stands experience the marching bands, cheerleaders and mascots. They hear the drum roll, watch as the flag is unfurled, and when it's fully displayed, the Star Spangled Banner is sung. These are electrifying and emotional moments in live sports events

This Is My Country

This is my country! Land of my birth!
This is my country! Grandest on earth!
I pledge thee my allegiance, America, the bold,
For this is my country to have and to hold.

What diff'rence if I hail from North or South
Or from the East or West?
My heart is filled with love for all of these.
I only know I swell with pride and deep within my breast
I thrill to see Old Glory paint the breeze.

With hand upon heart I thank the Lord
For this my native land,
For all I love is here within her gates.
My soul is rooted deeply in the soil on which I stand,
For these are mine own United States.

This is my country! Land of my choice!
This is my country! Hear my proud voice!
I pledge thee my allegiance, America, the bold,
For this is my country! To have and to hold.

Composed by Al Jacobs, lyrics by Don Raye

Scorecard: 2010s

U.S. Population	308 million
President	Barack Obama Donald J. Trump
Major Events	Haiti Earthquake (2010) Deepwater Horizon Explosion in Gulf of Mexico (2010) Osama Bin Laden Killed (2011) Occupy Wall Street protests (2011) Colorado and Washington Legalize Marijuana (2012) Boston Marathon Bombing (2013) Black Lives Matter protests (2015) Paris Climate Agreement (2016) #MeToo Movement gains momentum (2017) Trump Impeached (2019)
Most Popular Sport	Football
Sports Events	Boston Bruins win 1st Stanley Cup in 40 Years (2011) Derek Jeter Retires from New York Yankees (2014) U.S. Women's Soccer team wins World Cup (2015, 2019) Chicago Cubs win 1st World Series in 108 years (2016) Kobe Bryant Retires, 60 points in final NBA game (2016) Tom Brady and NE Patriots Win 6th Super Bowl (2019)

New Technology	Instagram (photo sharing) (2010) Apple iPad (2010) Uber (2011) Tesla Model S Electric Car (2012) Zoom video conferencing (2011) Amazon Alexa (2014) Apple Watch (2015) Internet of Things (IoT) (2015) Self-Driving Trucks (2017) 1st Photo of a Black Hole (2019)
Communications	Internet Television Social Media Radio
Average Baseball Ticket Price	$50.00

The Champions

MLB World Series

2010	San Francisco Giants	(4-1)	v. Texas Rangers
2011	St. Louis Cardinals	(4-3)	v. Texas Rangers
2012	San Francisco Giants	(4-0)	v. Detroit Tigers
2013	Boston Red Sox	(4-2)	v. St. Louis Cardinals
2014	San Francisco Giants	(4-3)	v. Kansas City Royals
2015	Kansas City Royals	(4-1)	v. New York Mets
2016	Chicago Cubs	(4-3)	v. Cleveland Indians
2017	Houston Astros	(4-3)	v. Los Angeles Dodgers
2018	Boston Red Sox	(4-1)	v. Los Angeles Dodgers
2019	Washington Nationals	(4-3)	v. Houston Astros

NFL Super Bowl

2010	New Orleans Saints	(31-17)	v. Indianapolis Colts
2011	Green Bay Packers	(31-25)	v. Pittsburgh Steelers
2012	New York Giants	(21-17)	v. New England Patriots
2013	Baltimore Ravens	(34-31)	v. San Francisco 49ers
2014	Seattle Seahawks	(43-8)	v. Denver Broncos
2015	New England Patriots	(28-24)	v. Seattle Seahawks
2016	Denver Broncos	(24-10)	v. Carolina Panthers
2017	New England Patriots	(34-28)	v. Atlanta Falcons
2018	Philadelphia Eagles	(41-33)	v. New England Patriots
2019	New England Patriots	(13-3)	v. Los Angeles Rams

NHL Stanley Cup

2010	Chicago Blackhawks	(4-2)	v. Philadelphia Flyers
2011	Boston Bruins	(4-3)	v. Vancouver Canucks
2012	Los Angeles Kings	(4-2)	v. New Jersey Devils
2013 *	Chicago Blackhawks	(4-2)	v. Boston Bruins
2014	Los Angeles Kings	(4-1)	v. New York Rangers
2015	Chicago Blackhawks	(4-2)	v. Tampa Bay Lightning
2016	Pittsburgh Penguins	(4-2)	v. San Jose Sharks

The Champions

2017	Pittsburgh Penguins	(4-2)	v. Nashville Predators
2018	Washington Capitals	(4-1)	v. Vegas Golden Knights
2019	St. Louis Blues	(4-3)	v. Boston Bruins

** Lockout cancellation of 510 games*

NBA Championship

2010	Los Angeles Lakers	(4-3)	v. Boston Celtics
2011	Dallas Mavericks	(4-2)	v. Miami Heat
2012	Miami Heat	(4-1)	v. Oklahoma City Thunder
2013	Miami Heat	(4-3)	v. San Antonio Spurs
2014	San Antonio Spurs	(4-1)	v. Miami Heat
2015	Golden State Warriors	(4-2)	v. Cleveland Cavaliers
2016	Cleveland Cavaliers	(4-3)	v. Golden State Warriors
2017	Golden State Warriors	(4-1)	v. Cleveland Cavaliers
2018	Golden State Warriors	(4-0)	v. Cleveland Cavaliers
2019	Toronto Raptors	(4-2)	v. Golden State Warriors

WNBA Championship

2010	Seattle Storm	(3-0)	v. Atlanta Dream
2011	Minnesota Lynx	(3-0)	v. Atlanta Dream
2012	Indiana Fever	(3-1)	v. Minnesota Lynx
2013	Minnesota Lynx	(3-0)	v. Atlanta Dream
2014	Phoenix Mercury	(3-0)	v. Chicago Sky
2015	Minnesota Lynx	(3-2)	v. Indiana Fever
2016	Los Angeles Sparks	(3-2)	v. Minnesota Lynx
2017	Minnesota Lynx	(3-2)	v. Los Angeles Sparks
2018	Seattle Storm	(3-0)	v. Washington Mystics
2019	Washington Mystics	(3-2)	v. Connecticut Sun

The Champions

NCAA College Football *

2010	Auburn		
2011	Alabama		
2012	Alabama		
2013	Florida State		
2014	Ohio State	(42-20)	v. Oregon
2015	Alabama	(45-40)	v. Clemson
2016	Clemson	(35-31)	v. Alabama
2017	Alabama OT	(26-23)	v. Georgia
2018	Clemson	(44-16)	v. Alabama
2019	LSU	(42-26)	v. Clemson

** Prior to 2014, the college football champion was determined by a combination of polls and/or committees.*
In 2014, it was replaced with the College Football Playoff (CFP), which utilizes a committee to seed teams.

Heisman Trophy

2010	Cam Newton	QB	Auburn
2011	Robert Griffin III	QB	Baylor
2012	Johnny Manziel	QB	Texas A&M
2013	Jameis Winston	QB	Florida State
2014	Marcus Mariota	QB	Oregon
2015	Derrick Henry	RB	Alabama
2016	Lamar Jackson	QB	Louisville
2017	Baker Mayfield	QB	Oklahoma
2018	Kyler Murray	QB	Oklahoma
2019	Joe Borrow	QB	LSU

NCAA College World Series

	Baseball *Men*	**Softball *Women***
2010	South Carolina (54-16)	* UCLA (50-11)
2011 *	South Carolina (55-14)	* Arizona State (60-6)
2012 *	Arizona (48-17)	Alabama (60-8)
2013 *	UCLA (49-17)	* Oklahoma (57-4)
2014	Vanderbilt (51-21)	* Florida (55-12)
2015	Virginia (44-24)	Florida (60-7)
2016	Coastal Carolina (55-18)	Oklahoma (57-8)
2017	Florida (52-19)	* Oklahoma (61-9)
2018	Oregon State (55-12-1)	* Florida State (58-12)
2019	Vanderbilt (59-12)	* UCLA (56-6)

**Indicates undefeated teams in College World Series play.*

NCAA College Basketball

	Men	***Women***
2010	Duke (35-5)	Connecticut (39-0)
2011	Connecticut (32-9)	Texas A&M (33-5)
2012	Kentucky (38-2)	Baylor (40-0)
2013	Louisville ** (35-5)	Connecticut (35-4)
2014	Connecticut (32-8)	Connecticut (40-0)
2015	Duke (35-4)	Connecticut (38-1)
2016	Villanova (35-5)	Connecticut (38-0)
2017	North Carolina (33-7)	South Carolina (33-4)
2018	Villanova (36-4)	Notre Dame (34-3)
2019	Virginia (35-3)	Baylor (37-1)

*** Title later vacated by Committee on infractions.*

Kobe Bryant

The 2020s

Into the Future With Intentional Optimism

As the ball fell at midnight in New York's Times Square to welcome 2020 to America, I couldn't help but reflect on my journey from the 1930s to that moment. Along with all of my fellow members of "The Silent Generation," we are now in our 80s with some in their early 90s. Thanks to lessons of life and the ***Intentional Optimism*** of our generation, we're still here and ***we made a difference!***

We had earned the right to enjoy our later years. For many of us, that meant more time to keep up with the sports world. As much as we had all seen sports grow through the years, none of us could have imagined how the dramatic effect of the rapid spread of the covid pandemic would impact the sports world.

As 2020 unfolded before us, we learned of a viral outbreak in China that had already spread to other countries. When cases began to appear in the United States, they were originally treated as some sort of "flu" outbreak. But as January turned to February, it became clear that this was something much more deadly. In late February, the Life Care Center in Kirkland, WA, recorded two deaths, believed to be the first in the United States. It soon became the "epicenter" of the outbreak in the United States as multiple deaths per day were reported.

In one of life's coincidences, I happened to be living just five miles from the Center and learned of the daily struggles of both residents and staff as well as first responders, initially through local and then national media as the death toll mounted.

On the sports front, as the pandemic raged across America through 2020, only the NFL managed to play a complete schedule. It took a tremendous effort to play the 256 game regular season schedule (plus playoffs), but play it they did. Cancellations led to a lot of rescheduling, but it worked, including the 2020 Super Bowl (February 2) and the 2021 Super Bowl (February 7). MLB, NBA, NHL, MLS, NCAA, as well as high school schedules were either canceled or greatly curtailed – and fans were barred from most games.

Interestingly, in the "everything old is new again" category, history repeated itself. (sort of). Recall that radio announcers in the 1930s and 1940s were not at the game sites. Rather, they literally simulated games using information transmitted by telegraph from the ballpark to the studio. But 90 years later - the 2020s - ESPN and other networks used the magic of today's technology (definitely NOT the telegraph) and had play-by-play and color analysts working from home or a remote studio while appearing to be at the game site. It was not uncommon to have a game in Florida, the play-by-play announcer in Colorado and the color analyst in Ohio! With that technology in the capable hands of very talented producers, directors, et al. – it all worked beautifully.

Meanwhile, you might be wondering what I was doing at the epicenter of the virus as it was unfolding literally "around the corner?" Well, on February 11, 2020, I was ordained so that I could officiate at my granddaughter Donna's wedding. The ceremony took place in Seattle on March 14, 2020. Had the wedding been scheduled for the following week, it wouldn't have happened because the Governor of Washington prohibited gatherings of more than ten people due to the rapidly spreading pandemic.

It was a little chilly, because it was held outdoors, so I wore an overcoat as two of my other granddaughters, Jessica and Sarah, escorted me down the aisle and up to the front. After the bridesmaids, Donna was accompanied by her parents, Lynn (my daughter) and Louie. And then the groom (Gavin) stepped forward. The entire ceremony was beautiful, just beautiful. I was surprised to learn afterward that, not only was the wedding filmed, but it was also streamed to our relatives who had to cancel their flights due to the pandemic. They were in five states, including: New York, Virginia, Texas, Florida, and Pennsylvania. They all watched it live and in full living color. While I was surprised that the new technology was being used for Donna's wedding, none of my grandkids were. What surprised them was that I was able get ordained to perform the ceremony. That was really cool, they thought. Then, in December 2021, my first great-grandchild was born. And I think that is pretty cool!

Looking back, I believe I've been fortunate to have seen technology change so much in my lifetime – from old-fashioned AM radio to the transistor radio to television to the iPhone to live streaming via the Internet [ESPN live streamed the first event in

The change in sports broadcasting technology I've seen in my lifetime is amazing

1995 - it was a baseball game]. The time has just flown by, which makes it seem to me that the growth has been phenomenal. And right along with it, I've seen the U.S. population increase from 125 million in 1932 to approximately 331 million in 2020. Of course, sports has grown right along with the populace and technology. When I was born, there were 16 Major League Baseball teams. Now there are 30. There were eight NFL teams. Now there are 32. There were 9 NHL teams. Now there are 32. And back then, there were no professional basketball leagues. Now there are 30 NBA and 12 WNBA teams.

Technology, I believe, enabled all this sports growth. It really began when RCA Americom launched the first domestic satellite, Satcom 1. We started ESPN with an uplink, not telephone lines – and typewriters, not computers. Over the years, I've had to explain to my youngest grandchildren what "typing" meant and what typewriters were. Now, they all "keyboard" using a computer or a mobile phone. And when I tell the ESPN story, I'm often asked how I kept going after being fired from the Whalers. "You have to be *optimistic* because life constantly wears you down," I say. "And you have to do it ***intentionally***." If I hadn't been fired, I probably never would have acted on the idea for ESPN. And even then, I was told so many times it would never work that a belief in myself and the optimism that I could make it happen kept me going. When I went looking for funding, I was turned down again and again. Regardless of all the "no's," all you need is one "yes," and you're in business. We pursued every potential investor. We were out of money and breathing our last gasp when we received that "yes" from Getty. Of course, Getty's greed in demanding 85 percent of the company was upsetting. But for me, personally, it wasn't so much about the money as it was about making a 24-hour sports network a reality. So we got it going, had a wonderful start, and experienced astonishing success. Then, a few years later, I was "retired" by the majority owners. I guess you could say that I was "let go" twice – once by the Whalers and once by the company I founded. Still, that's no reason to be pessimistic or passive. As I like to say:

"ABC - NBC:
Always **B**e **C**urious.
Never **B**e **C**omplacent."

Despite all the negativity encountered in the early days, I believe time has proven my instincts right. A natural impediment to creative new ideas is always rooted in the old guard – the men and women who, as they so often told me, "have been doing it this way for twenty-five years and don't see any reason to change." Team owners were unusually obstinate and said that if home games were broadcast, they would lose audience and fans. Cable owners were just as adamant that their businesses would lose revenue. Contrary to what they said, it was *because* of the exposure they received from ESPN that total viewership, the number of fans in stadiums and arenas, and revenue have all skyrocketed. Even so, there were many members of the old guard who still refused to change. As late as 2007, for instance, the Chicago Blackhawks were mired in the old-school, pre-free agency way of doing business.

Team owner, Bill Wirtz, carried on the old way of doing things after his father, Arthur, died. He would not televise home games and stuck stubbornly to an ancient ticket policy that kept team revenue down. As a result, the Blackhawks were always in financial trouble, were perennial losers, and hadn't won a Stanley Cup since 1961. But that all changed in 2007 when Bill passed away, and his son, Rocky, took over ownership of the team. Rocky immediately embraced new technology and very quickly transformed the Blackhawks into a profitable and elite team. And in 2010, after a 40-year drought, they won the Stanley Cup.

After a 40-year dry spell, my Chicago Blackhawks won the Stanley Cup

In 2007, the value of the Chicago Blackhawks was $179 million. In 2020, it was $925 million. In 1981, two years after ESPN was founded, the value of the Chicago Cubs was $20.5 million. In 2020, it was $3.2 billion. In 1979, Nolan Ryan became the first pitcher to earn over $1 million a year. In 2020, the average salary for a starting pitcher was $5.2 million, and seven pitchers made more than $30 million per year. Nearly everything associated with professional sports increased exponentially since that first satellite was placed in orbit above the Earth. ESPN was there at the beginning and has grown right along with it. Our goal in 1979 was to do 24-hour sports, which is 8,760 hours a year. In 2019, ESPN delivered 83,340 hours (equivalent to nine and a half years) of live sports on their various platforms. That translates into 24,749 live events via twelve channels (1 broadcast, 8 cable), two radio networks, and twelve digital platforms (including Facebook, Twitter, YouTube, ESPN+, and the ESPN app.) The first of its kind to have service on all seven continents, ESPN now reaches more than 69 countries and territories around the world. And SportsCenter is still here, averaging up to 115 million viewers each month. Wow! All that from an idea that everybody said wouldn't work.

When we launched ESPN in 1979, I was a month shy of my 47th birthday. On October 15, 2020, I turned 88. I don't think I ever could have suspected back then that the people of ESPN would become something of a second family to me. But it's true. When I shared the news that I had Parkinson's Disease, the company got behind me with total and unbelievable support.

apda AMERICAN PARKINSON DISEASE ASSOCIATION
Strength in optimism. Hope in progress.

ESPN awarded a grant to the American Parkinson's Disease Association (APDA). Then, when I became an awareness ambassador for the Michael J. Fox Foundation, the company again stepped forward and awarded grants to them. I find it both ironic and heartwarming that ESPN, the organization I helped give birth to, is now helping give me life in my struggle with Parkinson's. To use a favorite baseball expression, it seems like we have circled the bases together.

With Intentional Optimism, I work closely with the American Parkinson Disease Association and am an awareness ambassador for the Michael J. Fox Foundation

Everybody has good and bad days. It's the nature of life. On a bad day, I can say I'm going to give up – or I can say, "Wait a minute, I'm going to do something positive." Every morning, I have a game plan for the day. I always start with some form of physical exercise

– and the rest of the day, I'll exercise my brain. Those two things go hand-in-hand and one is just as important as the other. My neurologist, Dr. Gordon, suggested that I task myself with sitting down and writing a page a day about something. So I kept my brain active by writing this book. And not only was the doctor right, I have also found it to be a lot of fun.

In living with Parkinson's, I've made a conscious decision to make my first thought in the morning a positive one. It's an intentional type of optimism, so I have something to look forward to each day. And that kind of thinking, as the song from *Mame* goes, allows me to: *Open a new window. Open a new door. Travel a new highway that's never been tried before.*

When I look back and think about it, though, that's really nothing new for me. It's the approach I've taken my entire life – always looking forward to what's next, always optimistic that I can do anything I set my mind to, knowing that family is really the most important thing in life.

So as I step into the future, I believe there's still a lot to do. I've never been to a Super Bowl, or the Kentucky Derby, or a Stanley Cup playoff, or an CFP National Championship, or the College World Series. But now, if I don't want to put up with the crowds, I can share the experience by watching the live-action on all kinds of different platforms.

Ever since my grandfather first told me about the 1906 World Series between the Cubs and the White Sox, I have never lost my enthusiasm for sports. Because whether you're five years old or 88 years old – score tied, bases loaded, bottom of the ninth, best pitcher on the mound, and best hitter in the batter's box – is still as exciting as it ever was!

Scorecard: 2020s

U.S. Population	331 million
President	Donald J. Trump Joseph (Joe) R. Biden, Jr.
Major Events	Iranian Gen. Soleimani killed in U.S. air strike (2020) Worldwide Covid-19 Pandemic (2020-2022) Covid Nursing Home Outbreak in Kirkland, WA (2020) Antifa and BLM Nationwide Riots (2020-2021) Fastest "Vaccine" in History (SARS-CoV-2 coronavirus) Alleged Election Voter Fraud roils Nation (2020-2021) Washington, DC Capital Hill Rally/ Protest (January 6, 2021) Haiti Earthquake (2021) U.S. Military withdrawn from Afghanistan (2021) Hurricane Ida (2021)
Most Popular Sport	Football
Sports Events	Fans Restricted at all major Sports events (2020) MLB Short 60-game season (2020) NHL Short season – Bubble Playoffs (2020) NBA Short season – Bubble Playoffs (2020) WNBA Short season (2020)

	NFL only Sport to play complete schedule (2020) NBA Legend Kobe Bryant dies in helicopter crash (2020) Tom Brady wins 7th Superbowl (2021) Tokyo Summer Olympics postponed to 2021
New Technology	Giant LED Video wall (movie making) (2020) Neuromorphic Computing (next generation of AI) (2020) Remote Work (2020) Coronavirus "Vaccines" (2020-2021)
Communications	Internet, Social Media Television Radio
Average Baseball Ticket Price	$ 53.00

The Champions

MLB World Series

2020 *	Los Angeles Dodgers	(4-2)	v. Tampa Bay Rays
2021	Atlanta Braves	(4-2)	v. Houston Astros

** Short season due to pandemic.*

NFL Super Bowl

2020	Kansas City Chiefs	(31-20)	v. San Francisco 49ers
2021	Tampa Bay Buccaneers	(31-9)	v. Kansas City Chiefs
2022	Los Angeles Rams	(23-20)	v. Cincinnati Bengals

NHL Stanley Cup

2020 *	Tampa Bay Lightning	(4-2)	v. Dallas Stars
2021 *	Tampa Bay Lightning	(4-1)	v. Montreal Canadiens
2022	Colorado Avalanche	(4-2)	v. Tampa Bay Lightning

** Short season due to pandemic.*

NBA Championship

2020 *	Los Angeles Lakers	(4-2)	v. Miami Heat
2021 *	Milwaukee Bucks	(4-2)	v. Phoenix Suns
2022	Golden State Warriors	(4-2)	v. Boston Celtics

** Short season due to pandemic.*

WNBA Championship

2020 *	Seattle Storm	(3-0)	v. Las Vegas Aces
2021	Chicago Sky	(3-1)	v. Phoenix Mercury
2022	Las Vegas Aces	(3-1)	v. Connecticut Sun

** Short season due to pandemic.*

The Champions

NCAA College Football

2020 *	Alabama	(52-24)	v. Ohio State
2021	Georgia	(33-18)	v. Alabama

** Short season due to pandemic.*

Heisman Trophy

2020	DeVonta Smith	WR	Alabama
2021	Bryce Young	QB	Alabama

NCAA College World Series

	Baseball *Men*	**Softball *Women***
2020	*Canceled due to Covid-19*	*Canceled due to Covid-19*
2021	Mississippi State (50-18)	* Oklahoma (56-4)
2022	Mississippi (50-23)	Oklahoma (59-3)

** Indicates undefeated teams in College World Series play.*

NCAA College Basketball

	Men	***Women***
2020	*Canceled due to Covid-19*	*Canceled due to Covid-19*
2021 *	Baylor (28-2)	Stanford (31-2)
2022	Kansas (34-6)	South Carolina (35-2)

** Short season due to pandemic.*

Afterword

To all the fans who made my dreams come true

Is this heaven? Where the outfielder is in my field of dreams, the scoreboard works even when the lights go out, and the silent flight of a balloon passes the players on the field. Yes, dear fans, for me, this is heaven

My dreams for the future include:

- Scholarships for college students
- Activity Kit for people with Parkinson's
- Celebrating in ESPN's 50th Anniversary in 2029

Image Credits

Introduction

Bill in first grade, Grandfather Frank O'Connor, Bill at age 6, Bill Rasmussen personal collection
1906 World Series, public domain, fair use

1930s

Babe Ruth, MM photos
Heisman Trophy, ESPN Images
First televised baseball game, public domain, fair use

1940s

Ted Williams, Neftali
Bob Feller inducted, ESPN Images
Cadet commander, at bat, Bill Rasmussen personal collection

1950s

Willie Mays, Neftali
AD AID brochure, Bill Rasmussen personal collection
NBC, CBS, ABC old logos, public domain, fair use

1960s

Muhammed Ali, Neftali
Bill Rasmussen, Bill Rasmussen personal collection
Bert and Harry, public domain, fair use collection
Redmen Network, Bill Rasmussen personal collection
Baseball in the Berkshires, public domain, fair use
The San Jose Sharks vs. the Anaheim Dicks, credit Elliot Lowe

1970s

Hank Aaron, Neftali
WWLP flyer, Bill Rasmussen personal collection
WHA, Hartford Whalers, public domain, fair use
Joe DiMaggio, Willie Mays, ESPN Images
Satcom 1,TBS, HBO, Master Charge, public domain, fair use
UConn baseball field, ESPN Images
Getty, ESPN, CNN, MTV, Weather Channel, Motel sign, public domain, fair use

1980s

Hockey image, RuslanShevchenko
1979 Issue, CT Magazine, Bill Rasmussen personal collection
NCAA, Supreme Court, Oklahoma, public domain, fair use
Big Ten TV, RCM Sports, Bill Rasmussen personal collection
ESPN International, public domain, fair use
Sunday Night Football, Chris Berman on NFL Countdown, ESPN Images

1990s

Hockey illustration, vladirina32
Muhammed Ali, ESPN Images

Bill with Ali, Bill Rasmussen personal collection
Champions PGA Tour, public domain, fair use
Stadium Naples™ golf course, Bill Rasmussen personal collection

2000s
Tiger Woods, isogood
Mike Piazza, ESPN Zone, ESPN Images
George Bodenheimer, George George Bodenheimer personal collection
College Fanz Sports Network, Bill Rasmussen personal collection
College Fanz Scholarship Fund, public domain, fair use
David Ortiz, ESPN Images

2010s
Tom Brady, Debby Wong
Plaque, Original sign, Satellite dish with sons, Bill Rasmussen personal collection
Bristol, Connecticut campus, ESPN Images
ESPN mission statement, Lynn Daniels personal collection
Rasmussen family, Bill Rasmussen personal collection
NY Yankees, public domain, fair use
Cubs win world series, College Football Playoff trophy, ESPN Images
Bill in cafe, Lynn Daniels personal collection
Bill in opening night control room, 6 Presidents, ESPN Images
Bill with young reporters, Lynn Daniels personal collection
Flag, Bill with George Grande, Robin Roberts, George Bodenheimer, Bob Ley, Chris Berman, 33 of 80 original employees, ESPN Images
CableVision magazine, Bill Rasmussen personal collection
Original SportsCenter set, Bill with Mike Tirico, Jimmy Pitaro on original set, ESPN Images
ESPN 40th logo, public domain, fair use
Town Hall, ESPN Images
Fab 5, Mike Soltys personal collection
1st pitch, with staff, cake, ESPN Images
Bill meets Jimmy Pitaro, Mike Soltys personal collection
Scoreboard at Phillies, Heddy Bergsman
Bill at Yankee stadium, ESPN Images
ESPN important people: Carrie Brzezinski, Rosa Gatti, Dick Vitale, Lynn Daniels personal collection
Scottie Connel, Evan Baker, Jim Simpson, Bud Wilkinson, ESPN Images
First production truck, ESPN Images
Bill throws first pitch Phillies, Heddy Bergsman
Bill throws first pitch Seattle Mariners, Why Bristol quick draw, Bill Rasmussen personal collection
Bill on NFL studio stairs, Bill meets Mike Soltys, Lynn Daniels personal collection
Bill contemplating the campus growth, ESPN Images
Bill with employee, Lynn Daniels personal collection
Satcom 1, public domain, fair use
Satellite farm, ESPN Images
Original sign 1979, Bill at DePauw boulder 1950, 2017, Ubben Lecture, Bill ringing the Monon Bell, Bill Rasmussen personal collection
Lambda Chi Alpha centennial, Lynn Daniels personal collection

Chicago Charming Children 1938, Bill Rasmussen personal collection
Bill starts race in Mobile, with Kyle Benjamin, in Groton, with granddaughters, Lynn Daniels personal collection
Bill's patches, ESPN license plate, Bill Rasmussen personal collection
American flag football stadium fireworks, ESPN Images
NASCAR pre-race Bristol TN, Lynn Daniels personal collection

2020s

Kobe Bryant, kathclick
pager, iPhone, control center, Studio X, Stanley cup, ESPN Images
American Parkinson Disease Association; public domain, fair use
Bill Rasmussen, ESPN Images
Michael J Fox Foundation, MAME, public domain fair use

End matter

Field of Dreams, #1 Dad, ESPN Images
Sports Junkies Rejoice!, Bill Rasmussen personal collection

I was the biggest fan of my grandfather and this young boy has his Dad for a hero at the ball park

Also by Bill Rasmussen:

Sports Junkies Rejoice!
The Birth of ESPN

For More Information

www.espnfounder.com
www.espnfounder.com/parkinsonsawareness
www.espnfounder.com/books
www.espnfounder.com/contact
bill-rasmussen-speaker.com